TRAVIS L. SCOTT

Think Differently

How Recruitment Marketing Gets You Noticed Over The Noise

Copyright © 2020 by Travis L. Scott

All rights reserved. No part of this publication may be reproduced, stored or transmitted in any form or by any means, electronic, mechanical, photocopying, recording, scanning, or otherwise without written permission from the publisher. It is illegal to copy this book, post it to a website, or distribute it by any other means without permission.

Travis L. Scott has no responsibility for the persistence or accuracy of URLs for external or third-party Internet Websites referred to in this publication and does not guarantee that any content on such Websites is, or will remain, accurate or appropriate.

Designations used by companies to distinguish their products are often claimed as trademarks. All brand names and product names used in this book and on its cover are trade names, service marks, trademarks and registered trademarks of their respective owners. The publishers and the book are not associated with any product or vendor mentioned in this book. None of the companies referenced within the book have endorsed the book.

First edition

Cover art by Susanna Anderson
Editing by Brannan Sirratt

This book was professionally typeset on Reedsy.
Find out more at reedsy.com

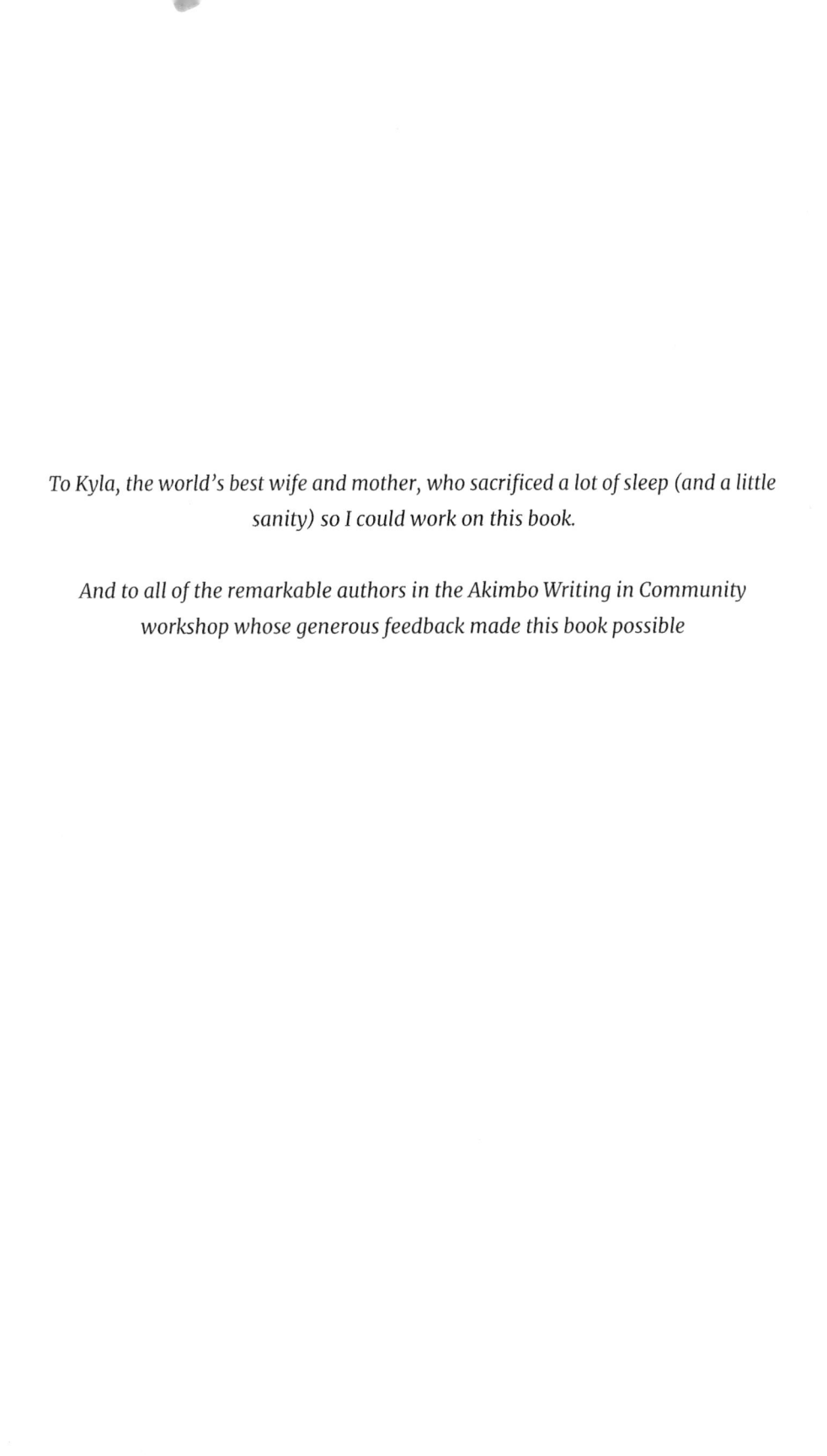

To Kyla, the world's best wife and mother, who sacrificed a lot of sleep (and a little sanity) so I could work on this book.

And to all of the remarkable authors in the Akimbo Writing in Community workshop whose generous feedback made this book possible

Contents

Foreword   vi
Acknowledgement   x

I   Part One

1   Introduction   3
2   Cognitive Entrenchment   6
     Marketers Facilitate Change, and You Need to Change   7
     The Middle is Missing   10
3   What Marketing Really Is   12
     Marketing Doesn't End with a Sale (or Hire)   15
     Marketing is Unselfish   16
     Knowing What Marketing Is Will Be Pivotal to Your Recruitment Marketing Career   18
     The Lure of MarTech   18
     "It's a Trap!"   20
     My View of Marketing Has Drastically Changed   21
4   It's ALL About People   22
     Marketers Serve   22
     We Market to People, For People   25
     Understanding Psychology and Sociology   26
     People are the Common Denominator – Creating Content for Your Audience   27
     Candidate Experience   30
     Customer (and Candidate) Experience - It Takes a Village   31
5   The Psychology of Marketing   34

	The Psychology of Marketing and Recruiting	34
	Marketing Portfolios and Maslow's Hierarchy of Needs	35
	Marketing, Human Behavior, and Maslow's Hierarchy of Needs	36
	Empathy	38
6	Knowing Who You're For (and Not For)	40
	Understanding Your Audience	40
	Newsflash: Chatbots aren't another job promotion mechanism	41
	Talent Networks Aren't Another Job Distribution Channel	41
	The Social Trap	42
	Understanding Your Audience	43
	Who You're Not For	46
	Going Beyond Job Postings	49
II	Part Two	
7	Moving Beyond the Old-School Mentality	53
	Wasting the Work	53
	The "Numbers Game" vs. The Minimal Viable Audience	55
	Your Minimal Viable Audience	58
	The (Long) Sales Cycle	61
	The Lure of Speed	63
	Wasted Opportunity	65
8	Funnels and Touchpoints	68
	Filling the Funnel	68
	Demographics are so Mid-20th Century	69
	Funnels and Touchpoints	70
	Funnels	70
	Touchpoints and Engagement	71
	Twin Funnels – Moving an Audience and Building an Audience	73
9	Focus on Who You're For, Understand Who You're Not For	76
	Competition and Positioning	76
	Purpose and Values	79

	Values	82
10	Internal Marketing	84
	Retention Rate and Replacement Costs	84
	Training, Learning, and Employee Retention	86

III	Part Three	
11	Focusing on the Wrong Things	91
	Spray and Pray Doesn't Work	91
	Recruiting is Essentially a Sales Role	93
	The Role of Technology in Recruiting	96
12	Where Do I Start?	98
	Where to Start	98
	The Lure of Automation	98
	Enter, Email Marketing	99
	You Already Have a Recruitment Marketing Team; You Just Don't Know It	102
	Start Small and Collaborate	103
	Human-Centered Design	105
13	Own Your Audience, Don't Rent It	109
	Four Reasons to Get Back to the Basics of Permission Marketing	109
	What Else Should You Be Doing?	113
	Permission Marketing: The Undisputed and Still Undefeated Champion of Modern Marketing	114
	Email Marketing – Still Overlooked and Still Effective	115
	They Want to Hear From You	118
14	Content Marketing	121
	Content and Brand Journalism	121
	Brand Journalism	122
	Content Creation	124
	What Will I Be?	125
15	Content Distribution and Inbound Marketing	128
	Long Sales Cycles and Risk	128

	Multi-Channel Attribution	130
	The Marketing Funnel	131
	The Candidate Journey	132
	Marketing Automation	136
	What is Marketing Automation	136
	How It Works	139
	Segmentation and Strategic Content Delivery	140
	Retargeting	143
	Benefits of Retargeting	144
	Retargeting and Recruiting	144
16	Measurement and Analytics	146
	An Introduction to Measurement	146
	Sales and Marketing Aren't Measured the Same So Why is Recruitment Different?	147
	Measurement – More Than Leads (Candidates)	148
	What to Measure – Using Marketing Analytics	151
	Using Marketing Analytics	152

IV Part Four

17	Becoming a Marketer and Building a Team	157
	A Marketer's Mindset	157
	Lack of Diverse Experience and Technology	160
	What If…?	162
	You Wouldn't Hire a Butcher to Be Your Five-Star Chef	163
18	The Future of Recruitment Marketing	168
	Is It Impossible or Just Difficult?	168
	The Biggest Opportunity that Exists in Recruitment Marketing Today	170
	Where will Recruitment Marketing Innovation Happen? Hint: Not Where You Think	171
	Recruitment Marketing and Employer Branding for Non-Enterprise Companies	174
19	Conclusion	176
	This Book is for Long-Term Focused Organizations	176
About the Author		178

Foreword

This book was written as part of the *Writing in Community* Akimbo workshop. It was an idea and experiment that was bravely put into the world by Kristin Hatcher to see if several hundred people could come together to write their books in an environment of generous peer feedback and support.

We began writing on the Summer Solstice, June 21, 2020. We were given the objective of publishing our books to the Kindle Direct Publishing platform by December 21, 2020, which happens to be the winter solstice.

I can now say I completed that objective and pressed the 'publish' button on Monday, December 21, 2020.

This is the first book I've ever written. In fact, I never thought writing a book was something I would ever do. But it's 2020. There are a lot of things many people thought they would never be doing that they've done during this crazy and unprecedented year.

Writing a non-fiction book was more challenging than I thought. Actually, the writing part was easy.

It was the mental aspects of writing a non-fiction book that I didn't expect.

"The Resistance" is a term that was coined by Steven Pressfield to describe the feeling we get when doing creative work. It occurs when we start talking ourselves out of writing. When we feel stuck or start to make excuses for why we're not the right person to write this book. How we tell ourselves it can be better.

I didn't think I would experience it. But I did.

It manifested itself in the form of perfection. I truly believe there are no such thing as an expert. There will always be people who know more than I do (and more than you know) about a topic. I've come to realize this and am dedicated to continuing to uncover the edges of various topics, mostly marketing-related, throughout the course of my career. This has also been a valuable weapon against Imposter Syndrome.

No one knows everything about anything.

That's what makes it difficult to write a non-fiction book. I was constantly learning something new. My perspectives would change.

This made me think that my book could be better.

What I realized is that it could always be better. Everything can be better in some way.

But, I was stuck and was determined to make it better. This thinking got me off track and began to derail my publishing goal along with my peers in the workshop on December 21st.

In late November, Kristin hosted a "Community Huddle" that Seth Godin was a part of. During the huddle, he implored us not to miss the December 21st deadline. To ship our work, even if doing so meant there would be partially written sentences.

Get it out into the world, he implored. Ship it. You can always make it better.

I had just begun working with an editor and was resolved to the fact that I wasn't going to publish my book until sometime in Q1 of 2021. I rationalized this by telling myself it was still earlier than the goal I had given myself at the beginning of 2020 to publish a book by April 17, 2021.

But that wasn't the point. That was a convenient place to hide.

Back in June, I had created a new shipping goal.

Hearing Seth talk about getting our work out into the world, combined with knowing that I can always update my book with a new edition, made me recommit to my initial goal of publishing on the Winter Solstice.

That's what I've done.

This book isn't perfect. It never will be.

There's still work to be done, including the insertion of stories and information I gathered through the interviews I conducted. I plan to continue working with my editor to make it better by revising and editing each chapter, incorporating the *Story Grid* method of editing and writing for non-fiction.

However, I made a commitment and I'm treating this like many technology companies treat their initial product launches - get a minimal viable product out into the world to be tested by its users. In my case, get it in my target audience's hands in hopes of receiving generous feedback that will make it better as I complete the editing phase.

So that's what I'm doing.

If you've purchased this book during this phase, I am truly appreciative and welcome any feedback you would be willing to share as I continue to work on the final edition.

Please send any feedback you have to me at:
travis@rainierdigital.com.

Acknowledgement

First and foremost, I want to thank my wife, Kyla, for being so patient with me throughout the writing of this book as well as the time I've spent in all of the other Akimbo workshops I've spent time with over the past year and a half.

Writing a book while also welcoming a new son into the world during a global pandemic has not been easy. Without in-person family support due to travel restrictions from the COVID-19 virus, it's been doubly hard.

I want to thank several people from the workshop who provided generous feedback and support throughout this journey: Lilian Mahoukou, Steven Price, Michael Feeley, Scott Perry, Michael Walsh, Kristin Hatcher, Louise Karch, Xiuming, and my Moose team - Annette Mason, Luke Harris, and Kelly Battaglia.

This book also would not have been possible without the generous time and perspective I received from the people I interviewed. Quotes, stories, and anecdotes from my conversations with them will appear in the next edition due to be released in March 2021.

A big thank you to those folks: Lory Sylvia, Allyn Bailey, Lars Schmidt, Katrina Kibben, Jody Ordioni, Adam Gordon, Brad DiPaolo, Emily D'Andrea, Brandy Ellis, Brian Smith, Carrie Corbin, Jodi Brandstetter, Bryan Chaney, Jenifer Dilapi, Ali Hackett, Amit Parmar, David Rivel, Ashley Walls, Peggy Saint-Auret, Angela Romei, and Erica Larson.

I also want to thank Regan Herberg for her help with some of the research.

I

Part One

1

Introduction

"It's hard to see the world in a new way when you're doing things in the same old way."
   - Dorie Clark, author of *Finding Your Breakthrough Idea*

When I first thought about writing this book and was coming up with reasons justifying the time I would spend, it was mostly for me.

It was to explore a nagging, underlying 'what if' that had been simmering just below the surface of my career consciousness.

As I get older, the weight of regrets seems heavier. I realize time isn't going to stop or slow down that the window for 'do-overs' becomes smaller.

Writing and using this book as a mechanism for decision making has been a good start.

What I've come to realize is when you are part of something bigger than yourself, beyond yourself, it becomes not only sustainable but potentially unstoppable.

There are several "why" questions anyone could ask me about this book:

- Why write this book?
- Why write it about recruitment marketing?
- Why am I the person to write it?
- Why would I start a business focused on it?

All of these questions have the same answer: To create a better experience and encourage creativity and a new way of thinking to challenge the old way of doing things.

First and foremost, to create a better candidate experience.

If marketing is done correctly, it helps people get what they want, desire, or need. This, in turn, helps a company get what they want.

Does a person really want to be hired at your company because of the salary? Or is it because of how it will make them feel about themselves and their career trajectory?

I also hope to create a better business experience. If marketing is done correctly, it aligns your product or service with the people it's best suited for. Not the masses.

Marketing is no longer about the 'numbers game' of flinging your message far and wide to as many people as possible, hoping 5% say 'yes'.

It means being efficient and effective, which creates a better candidate experience and a better process experience for everyone involved with hiring and interviewing at the company.

INTRODUCTION

The way hiring is done can be better.

The way hiring is experienced can be better.

For too long, companies have inwardly thought about themselves regarding hiring and the process involved.

It's time to think differently about recruiting. It's time to focus on the people who truly make your company remarkable - its current and future employees.

2

Cognitive Entrenchment

"Progress is impossible without change, and those who cannot change their minds cannot change anything." – *George Bernard Shaw*

We all know that Albert Einstein was a brilliant man. But it's interesting to note that his ideas and thoughts didn't just miraculously emerge from the ether.

He was intentional about exposing himself to a wide range of topics and ideas early and throughout his career.

At his core, he was an innovator. However, like most of us, early in his career, he needed a job.

However, I would venture to say that most of us were not as deliberate about the kind of job we chose as Einstein was.

He deliberately chose to work at a patent office. Why? So he could be exposed to a wide range of ideas.[1]

This would prove invaluable to the way he thoughts about new concepts.

You see, nothing in the world is new. The things we see as new are usually nothing more than the combination of things that already exist.

Marketers Facilitate Change, and You Need to Change

In its most simple form, marketing is the art and skill of making change happen.

I'll get into this in more detail later in the book, but I wanted to mention it now. After all, you're likely reading this because you are interested in changing yourself and your company's recruitment program.

To do this, you'll need to change the way you think and learn new concepts.

You've climbed the ranks and are now a leader in talent acquisition or recruitment within your organization.

You're where you are today because you're good at recruitment and HR.

Not because you're a marketing professional.

But now, you're beginning to feel pressure to do more beyond the traditional recruitment framework. You understand that the world changes fast, and the old ways of doing things either won't work forever or already are no longer relevant.

---

[1] https://en.wikipedia.org/wiki/Albert_Einstein

For one, the old ways of recruiting are expensive and, most of all, they're highly competitive.

You're searching for the same talent as everyone else. The waters you're fishing from are blood red.

How can you move to the blue water?

You realize, to find this blue water, you're going to have to change. This includes adding another layer missing from talent acquisition for some time, and I would argue it is still missing.

This layer is marketing.

But you don't have any marketing experience, and you realize no one on your team does either.

You likely got into recruitment early in your career and really didn't know anything else. You were taught by people who entered the same way, and they didn't really know anything else.

To compound this, you've hired similar people to your team and trained them the same way that you were taught. The cycle of entrenchment repeats itself.

If a long-time salesperson were asked to build their company's marketing program, they would likely struggle.

This is because marketing and sales are two different things with different timeframes and rewards, among other things.

Marketing and recruitment are no different.

"The secret of change is to focus all of your energy, not on fighting the old, but on building the new." - *Socrates*

So, why should a long-time talent acquisition professional be tasked with doing something a company wouldn't ask a sales professional to do?

I'll tell you why. It has nearly everything to do with your budget and the fact that talent acquisition is seen as a cost center by most companies.

This means, to build a recruitment marketing program, you're going to have to learn entirely new concepts. Most importantly, you're going to have to create a new lens or frame with which you view recruitment.

This kind of change is challenging.

There's actually a term in psychology for this inflexibility to changing situations and strategies called cognitive entrenchment.

Cognitive entrenchment is the decreased ability to change when you've been in a field too long. The longer you've been entrenched in an area, the less likely you will spend time exploring other fields. Therefore, your exposure to new ways of doing things and thinking is nonexistent.

Most things we think are new usually aren't. They're often a combination of two things that already existed that result in something 'new.'

When you don't expose yourself to new and different things outside of your current discipline, the likelihood that you will create something new dramatically decreases. Therefore, the possibility that something new will succeed in your organization also decreases. Because you don't have a frame of reference necessary to know what you don't know.

When it comes to recruitment marketing, those entrenched in the field are not exploring other disciplines.

They aren't going to marketing conferences. They may go to *recruitment marketing* conferences with speakers holding a similar career track as themselves.

I know this because I go to many marketing conferences, and I always scan the list of attendees and their titles to see how many recruitment marketing professionals are there. Usually, it's a handful to none.

The Middle is Missing

When a program is built, it's often created through the lens of recruitment, not marketing. Occasionally, a marketer is brought in to build the recruitment marketing program, but their experience isn't holistic, meaning they've either been a corporate brand marketer or have experience leading a company's social media presence.

This often leads to failure because these two things are only part of a marketing program and mostly focus on building awareness and driving leads. In terms of recruitment, leads can be viewed as applicants.

The entire middle section of what is known as the marketing funnel is missing and neglected.

This middle of the funnel is focused on building consideration, and it is where, if done correctly, companies can obtain the most significant competitive advantage.

You'll learn more about the marketing funnel later in this book, especially this area of fostering consideration, but first, let's focus on the core of what marketing is – and isn't.

3

What Marketing Really Is

Marketing may not be what you think it is. When many people who aren't in marketing think about what it is, they often go straight to what they see – TV commercials, big brand mass marketing, and big-city advertising agencies—the stuff of *Mad Men*.

It used to be, to sell your products or services, you needed to get exposure to as many people as possible. You needed to cast a wide net. Everything in marketing was about how to build a larger net.

The reason being, most marketing that was done was brand marketing. The thing about brand marketing is you don't always directly know how your monetary investment is performing. Measurement can be difficult.

Nowadays, nearly everything can be (and is) measured. We live in more of a direct marketing world.

The internet blew up how marketing used to work. On the surface, it may seem as though the internet gave us more reach, but in fact, it really gave us the ability to hyper-focus.

We no longer have to "spray" our message and "pray" that the message landed in front of the right people.

We now know where our audience lives online, how they think, and what's important to them. This is made possible because we're flooded with data points about our target audience through platforms like Facebook, LinkedIn, and Google.

Our ability to get our specific messaging in front of exactly the right audience at precisely the right time.

But at its core, marketing hasn't changed at all. It has always been about people.

In his book, *This Is Marketing*, Seth Godin defines marketing as "the generous act of helping someone solve a problem. Their problem. Marketing helps others become who they seek to become".

Think about that last part for a moment. "Marketing helps others become who they seek to become."

There's so much to that. A big part of marketing is understanding the role of status.

In our society, there are really very few things people need. Most of what we purchase has to do with what we want.

What most people want is to preserve or elevate their status among their peers or within their tribe. No one wants to buy something that will end up embarrassing them in front of those whose opinions they care about.

Every purchase has an internal story behind it. Even if you say you don't care about the kind of toothpaste you buy and only buy the cheapest, you're seeking to maintain the status you project of being a frugal person.

THINK DIFFERENTLY

The single biggest mistake companies make when it comes to marketing is thinking it's about themselves when, in reality, it's *all* about the customer and the problem they're trying to solve.

Recruitment marketing is no different. Instead of solving a customer's problem, you're solving a candidate's (and future employee's) problem.

They may realize that their career path has gone cold, or they're grossly underpaid compared to people doing the same thing at another company, or they're no longer learning and growing within their current role, or they want to choose the market and industry they work in because they're not passionate about the one they're in now. This list goes on and on.

Those are all problems. Problems a person is trying to solve that will improve their life. Can working for your company solve this person's career problem? Can you make their life better?

The answers to these questions involve making change happen.

Therefore, marketing is about making a change.

This could be changing someone's attitude or perception about something before and after they purchase a product or service or choose an organization to work for.

It could even be how, when, and where they buy something.

In his book, *What Do You Want Your Customers to Become?* Michael Schrage talks about innovation and how, to gain traction with a new product or service, a company must teach their customers how to use their product.

"Successful innovators don't just ask customers and clients to do something different; they ask them to become someone different," Schrage writes.

He continues by saying, " Successful innovators ask users to embrace—or at least tolerate—new values, new skills, new behaviors, new vocabularies, new ideas, new expectations, and new aspirations. They transform their customers. Successful innovators reinvent their customers as well as their businesses. Their innovations make customers better and make better customers."[2]

Marketing Doesn't End with a Sale (or Hire)

The funny thing about people's perceptions is that they can change at any time. Just because someone purchased something, it doesn't mean the same feelings they had before the purchase will continue indefinitely.

Because most people are in constant pursuit of "better," a brand, company, or organization must work even harder post-sale to maintain the customer's positive perception.

The competition will never go away and will relentlessly try to sow doubt in your customers' (or, in the case of recruitment marketing, your employees') minds. There will *always* be a choice, and your product, service, or organization isn't the only choice available.

How you treat your customer (or employee) after the sale (or hire) is the most profitable thing you could focus on as a company. Marketing doesn't end with the sale (or hire).

Broken promises can destroy your brand or company.

---

[2] [1] Schrage, Michael; Schrage, Michael. Who Do You Want Your Customers to Become? (p. 11). Harvard Business Review Press. Kindle Edition.

Marketing is Unselfish

Back in 2006, I graduated with an MBA from the University of Colorado. I went back to school because I had practically zero experience or understanding of the business world.

My undergrad degree was in Environmental Science.

I had no idea what I wanted to focus on in business, so I decided to get an MBA and learn about it all, hoping that something would resonate. And it did: marketing.

Back then, digital was still pretty new. iPhones didn't exist. Pay-per-click ads were basic and straightforward.

MySpace was the social media platform of choice.

So, I learned the basics. The old school, 7-P's basics. Basics from the likes of Philip Kotler. I learned about GAP and SWOT analyses.

My education was a great foundation, but things changed quickly after that. The Don Draper days of viewing advertising *as* marketing were coming to an end.

Sure, ads are still a valuable business. Especially for companies like Google and Facebook. It essentially pays their bills.

But modern marketing goes beyond only serving the company. It's more important than ever to focus on the customer, their needs, wants, and desires. Empathy is more important than tactics.

In modern marketing, empathy for the customer guides everything you do –

from your messaging to the customer experience pre-, during, and post-sale, to the tactics you employ.

Modern marketing is unselfish. This unselfishness is why I was so happy to see that recruitment marketing is a thing. The possibility now exists to create a great candidate *and* employee experience like never before.

The possibility to put candidates first. Not metrics based on the number of hires made. Not the checking of boxes. But, instead, the possibility to truly understand who is happiest at your company, who performs their best at your company, who is willing to tell others about how great it is to work at your company.

Gone should be the days of measuring a recruiter's effectiveness based on faceless numbers.

What should be measured is candidate experience – including the experience of those who didn't get hired.

Just as marketing's role should not end after the sale, recruitment marketing should extend beyond the hire. A partnership with HR should be established to ensure open communication with employees to improve their experience and happiness and help grow their careers and nurture their professional growth.

Knowing What Marketing Is Will Be Pivotal to Your Recruitment Marketing Career

Truly understanding what marketing is (and isn't) will be critical to the work you do as a marketer. Society, and to some extent, industries, like to box things up and place labels on them. Group them in a way that makes sense. Problems arise when barriers are built around these things and are impervious to new ideas or the reality that cross-over exists.

The bulk of my marketing experience has been B2B marketing. Sure, there are some nuances between B2B and B2C marketing, but not as many as a lot of marketers think. They also tend to create a narrative that they are vastly different, and because a certain tactic or strategy was used in a B2C context, it doesn't apply to B2B.

The same could be said for recruitment marketing. There are certainly some unique elements to recruitment marketing, but there are many more elements of B2B *and* B2C marketing that it has in common than those that are different.

Having a solid marketing foundation will be crucial to your ability to vet marketing technology and truly understand how it can become a beneficial lever to your underlying strategy and team. Not the other way around.

This is a trap many marketers fall into, especially early in their careers.

The Lure of MarTech

During my time in marketing, MarTech (marketing technology) has exploded.

When I got my MBA in marketing from the University of Colorado at Denver from 2003 to 2006, marketing technology was in its infancy.

MySpace dominated social media.

Yahoo! was still a widely-used search engine. However, the titanic change was underway. Google's search engine was gaining traction.

Google Ads (known then as Google AdWords) and Google Analytics were born during this time. But "optimizing for mobile" wasn't even a thing because the iPhone hadn't been invented yet.

Philip Kotler, the "Father of Modern Marketing," was an influential part of my education. His books were our textbooks.

While much of what Kotler has taught us remains true today, we also learned the old school stuff like Jerome McCarthy's 7 *Ps of Marketing* that he developed in the 1960s.

We learned about SWOT and Gap analyses, as well as Michael Porter's *Five Forces* framework.

When I graduated in 2006, I left with a solid understanding of marketing – at its core.

Since then, digital marketing has become a billion-dollar industry, with MarTech (marketing technology) being a huge part. According to a report by BDO, WARC, and the University of Bristol, worldwide spend on MarTech is expected to reach $121 billion in 2019, with $65.9 billion coming from North America and the UK alone.[3]

That's a staggering figure. Especially given, it was barely even a thing 15 years

---

[3] https://chiefmartec.com/2019/10/martech-now-121-5-billion-market-worldwide/

ago.

"It's a Trap!"

This appetite for technology has become a trap, though. Instead of being seen as a lever to be used within a more broad marketing strategy based on people and psychology, MarTech sometimes becomes the strategy.

It has become a shortcut and a crutch from doing great marketing. It has put metrics at the front of marketing instead of the people we seek to serve. We now market to metrics. Not people.

It was easy to get caught up in new technology that could make your life easier as a marketer. Tech that could help you reach more people. Which, my flawed thinking told me, was the surefire way to get more leads. This is a classic sales and recruiting way of thinking. As I've mentioned, it's also an old-school marketing way of thinking – cast a wide net and sort the fish. The goal is always to be building a bigger net. Fishing with a spear is much more efficient once you know where the lake's best place to fish is.

However, this is no way to gain a competitive advantage. Instead, you're simply doing what everyone else is doing.

Now, I'm not saying that technology and metrics aren't great. I'm not saying that I long for the pre-digital days. I don't. In fact, I think there has been no better time to be a marketer than today.

I'm saying that I, like many in the field, lost my way and became too enamored by the tech and forgot about what marketing truly was.

Having a tech-first strategy is also expensive. It didn't become a $121 billion industry by giving things away.

My View of Marketing Has Drastically Changed

Then, in 2019, I enrolled in Seth Godin's Akimbo workshop, *The Marketing Seminar,* and everything changed for me.

I was able to get back to the basics of marketing. Back to the core of what marketing truly is – a way to make change happen and serve those you seek to serve.

It's not about technology. It's not about analytics. Over the course of 100-plus days, we didn't learn a single thing about MarTech. We didn't even talk about analytics.

We learned about empathy, psychology, how ideas spread, enrollment, and storytelling. It was *all* about people.

This changed everything for me. After a decade of digital marketing experience, my world was flipped upside down.

And it has made all of the difference in the world.

This new perspective is what drove me to explore the topic of recruitment marketing. It's what drove me to write this book, and it's what is driving me to share this perspective and way of doing marketing the right way with my peers in the industry to create a better way to recruit and retain employees. To create a better experience for the candidate. Something long overdue.

4

It's ALL About People

Marketers Serve

The products or services a company sells are designed to solve a problem.

As people discover their problems, they enter into a phase within what's known as a marketing funnel.

In its simplest form, the AIDA marketing funnel model developed by Elias St. Elmo Lewis includes four stages: Awareness, Interest, Desire, and Action.[4]

---

[4] https://www.smartinsights.com/traffic-building-strategy/offer-and-message-development/aida-model/

```
         Awareness
          Interest
           Desire
                    ← Action
```

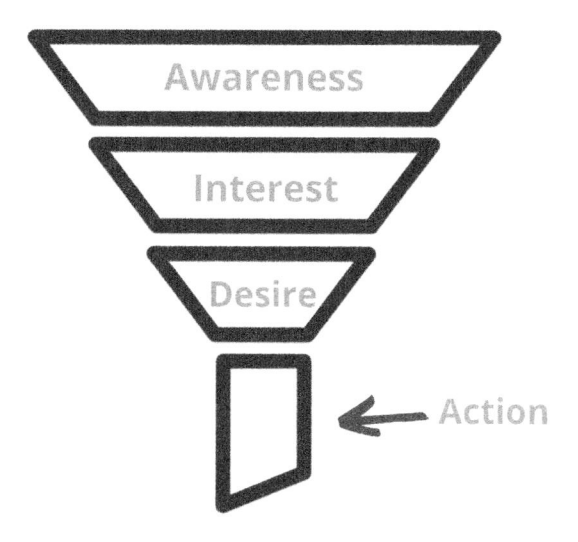

This has since evolved to include post-sale activities such as loyalty and customer advocacy.

A marketer's objective is to serve people as they enter and move through various marketing funnel levels.

At the Awareness phase, they introduce their product or service to the person, making them aware of their offering as an option to solve their problem.

They follow this up by serving useful information about features and benefits compared across other similar competitive offerings during the Interest phase.

This can be done by offering case studies, blog posts, and whitepapers, among other things.

Every activity up to (and after) these two phases builds trust and works to create an emotional bond between the prospective customer and brand. Making, or insinuating, promises along the way, as I mentioned earlier in the book.

When someone moves into the Desire phase, they've made an emotional connection with your brand. This is where the results of tension and status employed during the Interest phase begin to pay off by moving the person from merely being interested in your product or service to now wanting it. You've made a promise (or several). Expectations are now set.

The final stage, Action, is the point at which the person purchases your product or service. As a marketer, you serve the prospective customer by creating a clear and understandable way for the purchase to happen. This is often referred to as providing a "call to action" or CTA. Which at this stage, the Action is the purchase.

CTAs can also be used in previous stages depending on the Action the prospective customer would need to take next. Examples could be to watch a pre-recorded demo, request free samples, get pricing or a quote, or download a whitepaper.

At every step of the way, marketers serve people what they want, when they want it, and how they would like to receive it.

In many cases, they continue to serve people even after becoming customers by developing useful information about using and getting the most out of the product or service by providing updates on new designs or features, communicating issues or bugs. The list goes on and on, but they continue to build trust and brand equity among their customers by serving their needs.

Are customers and prospects the only people marketing serves?

Nope. They also serve the company's sales team, the customer service team, and others within the organization. In a way, recruiters serve multiple people as well – candidates and the hiring managers whose open roles they intend to fill.

We Market to People, For People

Marketing is at the heart of all that we do. If you aren't involved in business, you still are engaged in some kind of marketing – at some point in your life.

If you've had to educate someone, or you talked about a product you just purchased, or you needed to get the word out about a party you were having, you were marketing.

In doing so, we've marketed to people.

Marketing isn't solely about money being exchanged. Marketing is the catalyst for change.

One of the most misleading concepts in business is the term B2B or business-to-business. We say that we either do B2B marketing or B2C (business-to-consumer) marketing.

That, to me, dehumanizes what we do as marketers.

When you're marketing a product or service used in a business setting, you still have to market to a person within that business.

All marketing is H2H – human-to-human.

When you create change through marketing, you change the *way* people get something or change *what* they want.

Understanding Psychology and Sociology

It's always been interesting how many people leave college with a degree in Psychology or Sociology. The business world's perception is that those degrees are not very valuable compared to a business degree or computer science degree.

I would argue the contrary. I think both degrees could be more valuable than a business degree or computer science degree.

Take Facebook, for example. Software Engineers are probably put on a pedestal there, just like they are in every other tech organization. However, the psychology principles the platform is built on keeps people coming back day after day, sometimes hour after hour.

What the engineers did was what they were told.

They are, more or less, cogs in the system.

You can graduate with a business degree and understand accounting principles, statistics, management practices, operations, and marketing. Still, all of that isn't very helpful unless someone in your organization truly understands psychology and sociology.

If I were starting college over again and had to decide where I would spend my time – knowing that I would be pursuing a career in marketing – I would major in marketing and minor in both psychology and sociology. I would also take every creative-based elective I could, such as Art History.

People are the Common Denominator – Creating Content for Your Audience

When it comes to marketing – recruitment marketing or otherwise – there's one common denominator to it all: people.

As I've mentioned, if you're a marketer, you're trying to affect some kind of change — most of the time, that change has to do with a person's behavior or perspective.

When people come across something new, the typical (and subconscious) reaction is to compare it to something they already know.

They think about a problem they have and measure up the effectiveness of your solution.

People always have a problem. It can be a legit problem, like their refrigerator is empty, and they need to buy more food.

Their 'problem' could be a low status among friends or colleagues.

A candidate's 'problem' could be a lack of challenge and fulfillment in their current role.

It could be they feel underpaid or undervalued.

They also could be happy in their current role with their current company.

But, they're interested in learning more about your company, the work culture and environment, the challenges involved, and the potential increase to their status.

Changing someone's mind about a life-changing event such as changing jobs or companies doesn't happen overnight, especially if they're currently happy or content.

They may realize, though, that their current company doesn't offer the long-term growth or career path they will eventually want, or the type of work they could be doing at your company seems interesting to them.

Are you currently happy in your current role at your current company?

If so, what other companies have sparked your interest? What would you want to know before you considered them a serious option? One that would make you contemplate leaving your current company.

Now, think about how that could be different for someone else. And someone else. And someone else.

You get it. People change jobs and companies for many personal reasons.

Sometimes they're rational reasons. Sometimes, they're irrational.

The good news, you have a lot to work with.

The bad news, you have a lot of work to do.

Before you create any more content, take some time to map out the different reasons someone would leave their current employer to work for you.

Having trouble coming up with reasons?

Interview recent hires, asking them why they chose to move to their team or the company.

Interview people who moved into a new role a few years ago. Why did they make a move?

Ask them to be honest with you about whether there has been a gap in what they expected when they joined the team or company. Has it been better or worse than they expected? Would they do it again, knowing what they know now?

Interview people who have recently left your company. Why did they leave? What did their new company promise that they weren't finding at your company?

Was there a mismatch in expectations, or did something change over time to misalign with their initial reason for joining your company?

Design questions that your recruiters can ask during their phone interviews.

The most important thing you can do as a marketer is to understand the psychology behind why people make the decisions they make- especially the decisions to choose (or not choose) your role, team, or company.

Doing this will give you insight and clarity into people's behavior. It will help you understand who your company is for and, just as importantly, who you're not for.

This will help you develop a strategy around the type of content you need to create, promote, and share.

Keeping in mind that the objective of your content is to communicate who you're for. Just as much as it's to communicate who you're *not* for.

Not everyone will want to work at your company. That's completely fine. In fact, wouldn't it be better that they figured this out before you spent the time interviewing them? There's an opportunity cost in everything, and interviewing someone who could have self-selected out prevents you from using that same time to interview someone you are for.

Candidate Experience

As I was writing this book, I happened to listen to a podcast on recruitment marketing. The hosts talked about candidate experience and how everyone realizes how awful it is, but nothing is done about it.

One of the hosts couldn't figure out where the gap was in terms of why there isn't more focus on this as a metric.

The topic of candidate experience is a meaningful one for me.

Here are my thoughts on this: a) how positive would you be if you were told "you're not good enough" and then asked, "how'd you like that?" and b) it's never measured and, if it is, it's not weighted appropriately.

Until candidate experience metrics are weighted as equally as the other sales or recruiting- metrics like number of emails sent out, number of phone interviews scheduled, number of interviews, and number of hires- it will never matter and will always suck.

A leader in the organization may ask, "how does something like the candidate experience scale?"

Well, if a candidate has a bad experience, they certainly aren't going to refer other people to your roles, especially the ones that are the most talented, because their status would go way down with that person if they did.

If they have a good experience, they may be more inclined to apply to another role that they're actually an even better fit for in the future. Not to mention, they will gladly refer people or, at least, talk about how the experience was so much better than it was when they interviewed for a competitor's role.

Trust me. It scales just fine.

I also think candidate experience is a big gaping hole in recruitment marketing that needs to be addressed. Let's say a candidate is nurtured for a couple of years through an RM program, and they have had a positive experience. They're then handed off to a recruiter that treats them like any other candidate, and the recruiter ends up 'ghosting' them. All of the work up to that point will have been wasted.

A bad candidate experience is also a bad brand experience, and I'm honestly amazed at how little attention this gets from companies' marketing and branding departments. Bad recruiters ruin the hard work a company brand team has done in a matter of one email (or a lack of an email).

It's time to focus on metrics that allow us to measure candidate sentiment and experience. It's simply too important to ignore.

Customer (and Candidate) Experience - It Takes a Village

If you ask most marketers, "what's the most important KPI or metric you track?" you'll likely hear the same answer: revenue.

Why am I talking about revenue when recruitment doesn't directly generate revenue?

It's because revenue is the primary objective of every business – even nonprofits. Without it, the company couldn't survive, let alone grow.

This means it's the primary objective of every marketing program. The problem is it can be challenging to measure effectively due to the complexity of touchpoints and attribution in digital marketing, especially when a long sales cycle is involved.

Lifetime value, or LTV, is a critical measurement that doesn't reflect back on marketing enough.

However, all of these measurements rely on more than just marketing.

The entire organization must be on the same page when it comes to the pre-customer and customer experience. Marketing can drive all of the qualified leads in the world, but if the sales team is inept and provides a bad experience, then it doesn't matter.

If the product or service doesn't meet the customer's expectations, it doesn't matter.

The two critical denominators in ensuring a remarkable and consistent experience are shared values and a clearly articulated vision from the top.

The same is true with hiring and employee retention.

The employer brand team can paint the most attractive picture of what it's like to work at your company, and the recruitment marketing team can nurture someone who could be a remarkable employee. Still, if the recruiting team treats them like another transaction, delivering an awful experience doesn't matter.

If the role and company don't line up with what was portrayed in the nurturing and recruitment phases, and they end up leaving within six months or a couple of years, then it doesn't matter.

This is the same whether your objective is revenue or quality hires.

At the end of the day, it's all about people, specifically candidates and employees, and how they're treated.

Empathy is one of the most important traits a professional can possess, especially in candidate-facing roles such as employer branding, recruitment marketing, and recruitment.

5

The Psychology of Marketing

The Psychology of Marketing and Recruiting

The purpose of understanding psychology when it comes to marketing and recruiting is to better understand how people make decisions.

Marketing and recruiting involve people and the decisions they ultimately make.

In marketing, these decisions can happen as soon as a person sees an ad. They quickly determine if the brand is known to them or not. If it's not, people use heuristics or mental shortcuts to make decisions quickly, using as little cognitive energy as possible.

Their mind quickly tries to associate this new brand with something that is known. I've heard Seth Godin refer to this as "what does it rhyme with." They do this, both with the brand image being presented and the thing that is being sold.

Someone who is looking for a job or who receives an email from a recruiter telling them about an open role does the same thing.

Do they know the company? If not, what does it remind them of?

Is the job title something they've seen before? Is it similar to what they're doing now or want to do? If not, they subconsciously think, "what does it remind me of?" as they read the requirements within the job description.

In another scenario, they may have had a bad experience with a recruiter in the past, so merely receiving the email may cause an adverse reaction.

Heuristics can be a good thing as we go about our day, but they can often lead to poor decision making when it comes to urgent or complex decisions. This can also be true when it comes to things that are different than what we've experienced in the past, and we don't have a viable or comparable anchor for it.

Psychology is such an important part of marketing, I'm going to do a quick dive into some concepts that directly apply to marketing. Understanding these concepts will radically change the way you view marketing and the importance of recruitment marketing.

Marketing Portfolios and Maslow's Hierarchy of Needs

I recently heard someone refer to strategy as "the many battles you need to focus on to win the war."

This also could be used to describe modern marketing.

Just like the consumer journey is comprised of multiple and numerous touchpoints, so is the candidate journey.

I see so much emphasis on employer branding, with social media as the cornerstone. Marketing is much, much more than this. But I feel these are the two things that are both sexy and most visible to people who aren't marketing professionals.

Modern marketing is like a portfolio consisting of content development, email marketing, lead nurturing, SEO, paid media such as pay-per-click ads, display ads, and paid social, organic social, webinars, podcasting, blogging, among other things.

Marketing, Human Behavior, and Maslow's Hierarchy of Needs

As I've discussed ad nauseam to this point, at its core, marketing is about people and, specifically, human behavior and feelings. Most often, irrational behavior. Things like status, fear of missing out, comfort, safety, challenge, and self-actualization.

Unlike a lot of marketing that's focused on things people want, but likely don't need, a career or job is both a need and a want.

It's a need because, without income, life would be tough. For some people, they are only in need of a job.

It's a want because most people want to be happy with what they're doing, whether it's just a job or it's their career.

I'm a big believer in Maslow's Hierarchy of Needs and our desire to continue moving up the pyramid.

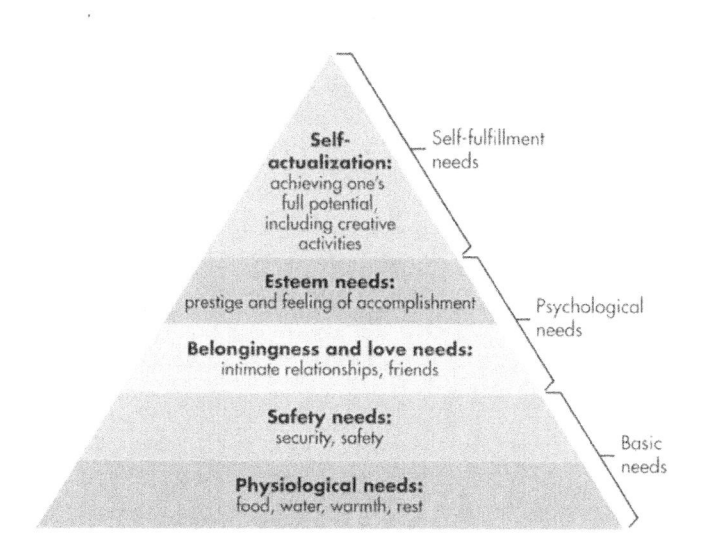

Fig. 1. – Maslow's Hierarchy of Needs

Even if we're looking for a job, we at least want to know that we'll stay where we are in terms of the Hierarchy of Needs and, many times, are hoping it will allow us to transition to the next level.

There are times, like what we're experiencing at the time I'm writing this book in 2020, in which people sometimes are forced to move down to a lower level to get by.

Someone who may have been at the 'Esteem' level before COVID-19 may now find themselves at the 'Safety' level looking for a decent job, any job, that will keep them from defaulting on their mortgage and able to provide for themselves or their families.

It's essential to understand people and what's going on in the world around us to be an effective marketer.

Let's use Disney as our example. Someone who may be looking for a low-skill, lower-paying role at one of Disney's theme parks likely has different needs and wants than someone looking to join the company as a Director of Marketing. They both want to be happy and feel like they're working toward something; however, one may be more concerned with job security, stability, college reimbursement, and excellent health benefits.

Understanding this is crucial to crafting the right messaging that will not only get someone's attention but will land emotionally with them.

Empathy

Great marketers (and leaders) are empathetic.

Empathy: it's a word that's used so much nowadays that you would think those in leadership roles within companies would have it nailed.

You would think everyone in business would have a crystal-clear understanding of what it is.

But they don't.

It seems the only empathy the leaders within companies have is toward their shareholders. Many of whom they don't even know.

Read nearly any job description posted out on Indeed or LinkedIn.

Does it read like the person who wrote it is curious and interested in how they can help the person who eventually fills that role achieve their wants and dreams as it relates to their career?

Or does it read like a laundry list of bullet points explaining how this person would fit into *their* culture and what *they* expect of this person?

Not a thing about what the person coming into this role can expect of the company, its leadership, or this person's future peers.

Do you really think people decide to join a company or team because their number one priority is helping that company's shareholders?

Do you think they come into a role thinking, "I want to work long hours, miss out on my kids' sporting events and plays so I can ensure my manager gets a promotion."

Hell no. So why do we expect this of them?

If you say empathy is essential and that your employees are what drives your success, then why do your actions not match your words?

Or is it just one of those "do as I say, not as I do" sort of things?

How inspiring is that?

And you wonder why it's so challenging to find great people to work at your company.

6

Knowing Who You're For (and Not For)

Understanding Your Audience

The book I'm writing is focused on diving into the often overlooked and underutilized concept of candidate nurturing.

Part of my research involves a lot of reading. I want to understand what's going on in the market now.

What's the mindset of recruitment marketing practitioners?

What real marketing strategies and channels are being implemented to nurture candidates?

I'm finding a ton of missed opportunities, starting with an overall lack of awareness around the audience.

I keep seeing mentions of using email to promote "resume writing tips" and using chatbots to promote jobs to someone visiting your career site.

Newsflash: Chatbots aren't another job promotion mechanism

Sidebar, I've been advocating using chatbots for quite a while, but not to promote jobs. These people are already on your career site. They don't need help finding your jobs. They need an easier way to apply. That's what chatbots should help with.

Use it as a way to get their email address so the chatbot can send the job to their email so they can apply later – especially if the visitor is on a mobile device.

Many companies still struggle with creating an easy way to apply to a job via mobile.

If they're on their mobile device, they likely don't have their resume nearby. There's also a chance they need to update their resume or LinkedIn profile before applying.

Why not make it easier for them to apply later?

The chatbot gathered their email address, so now they can go into an automated email sequence that reminds them to apply if they don't do so within the first 24 hours.

Talent Networks Aren't Another Job Distribution Channel

This is just an example of companies not understanding their audience, and it comes down to empathy.

Why would someone join your talent network? To get job updates?

Maybe. But not likely.

This may be shocking to some recruiters; not everyone is looking for another role.

That doesn't mean they're not thinking about their next move, but that next move may not be for a couple of years.

This is the timeframe a talent network should be operating against.

Calling it a "talent network" is a nice way to promote it externally, but internally it should be your nurturing list. A highly segmented and strategic, long-term nurturing list.

That person who declined your offer to go somewhere else? They should be invited.

The Social Trap

Email is your most valuable nurturing tool. Not social media. You really want to rely on an algorithm to ensure your message gets in front of the right people? Are you going to pay to distribute that message? Because organic social reach is atrocious. You'll be lucky to get in front of 10% of your audience, and good luck, ensuring that 10% are the real gems of your network.

As I get into my research, I'm finding a large emphasis on employer branding and not as much on recruitment marketing.

I want to know why because, in my opinion, recruitment marketing is much more valuable and has a much higher ROI than branding.

Branding is easy. It's easy to blast out your message and hope someone hears it. There's not a lot to measure when it comes to branding, so it's also easy to get off the hook.

Recruitment marketing, like most direct marketing, should be measurable. There's built-in accountability with recruitment marketing.

When done correctly, recruitment marketing takes time. Employer branding establishes trust and drives awareness.

Recruitment marketing upholds the promises of that branding and builds trust.

Recruitment marketing is an exclusive look inside your company, your teams, and the type of impactful work you're doing.

Recruitment marketing is *not* another job distribution channel.

Recruitment marketing is *not* a place to learn how to write your resume.

Recruitment marketing *is* a way for someone to decide if your company and your team is the type of place she wants to *be*.

Recruitment marketing *is* a long-term strategy.

Understanding Your Audience

This, to me, is one of the most important cornerstones to effective and successful marketing. Yet, it's often overlooked or glazed over because tools exist to make things easy and provide shortcuts.

We don't have to really know what motivates our audience to switch brands or decide it's time to purchase your product or service. We have tools that can advertise or get our message out in front of thousands of people.

Surely, enough will click and be interested, right? Why not play the numbers game and saturate the market?

One problem (among many) with this approach is it's expensive. Not just to your budget, but your brand.

If people see your brand over and over again and realize you're not for them, they'll eventually tune you out. They could even start to dislike your brand because they're sick of seeing it, especially when it doesn't apply to them.

When I was a software engineering recruiter on the Microsoft Windows team from 2013-2014, I often went head-to-head with Amazon. Back then, Amazon had a reputation for being an extremely demanding and emotionally-draining place to work.

In August 2015, a year or so after I left Microsoft, the New York Times published a scathing story that described what many of us already knew.

It didn't take a New York Times article to get the word out to recruiters, especially those in the Seattle area. We knew about this well before the article was published, and I used this to my advantage in several ways.

If I found out a candidate I was speaking with valued work-life balance, I would talk about the differences between Amazon and Microsoft when it came to this value.

All tech companies are mostly inadequate when it comes to work-life balance, but I will say that Microsoft is among the best when it comes to this.

I also knew that Amazon lured people with the promise of their stock, which was on a pretty serious upward trajectory at that time. To earn the maximum in stock, you had to stay long enough for it to vest. This is how they were able to keep so many employees around for so long, despite difficult working conditions. This is often referred to as "golden handcuffs."

Given this, I knew that people who had only been there about six months could be lured away. They hadn't spent enough time to vest anything and saw the writing on the wall.

However, if someone had been there for about one or two years, I wouldn't even contact them because I knew they couldn't walk away at that point and risk wasting the time they had spent accruing toward their vesting period. They wanted to suck it up for a few more years, get their money and leave.

Another example of understanding the market and my audience also took place when I was at Microsoft. There was a company based in Madison, Wisconsin, called Epic Systems.

I knew they were really good at hiring talented engineers who had recently graduated from college. The roles I mostly worked on required at least 2-3 years of professional experience, making Epic a great place to look for people.

I also knew that most of the people they hired right out of school were from the University of Wisconsin or other schools in the region. Not only were a lot of these engineers ready to make a move professionally, but many were also looking to experience a new geographic area, and Seattle is typically an easy sell to people in the upper Midwest, especially in the winter.

By understanding the market and my audience, I could be more deliberate and intentional about how I worked, who I targeted, and the messaging I used.

For example, I would *always* open my conversations with engineers during

January and February with small talk about the weather so they could see the difference, and I used it as a selling point.

Who You're Not For

Salespeople often talk about filling the "funnel" and in recruiting, it's referred to as a "pipeline."

Both concepts and terms come from the same line of thought: cast a wide net, pull in as many people as possible and sort it out later.

This is a flawed way of thinking. It not only creates more work for everyone involved, but it's also expensive and creates a negative experience for many of the people who have found their way to your "funnel" or "pipeline."

In digital marketing, there's a term used to describe the attraction and subsequent acquisition of people into the funnel: inbound marketing.

In recruiting, one form of this would be the use of job postings. Some inbound purists only consider permission marketing done through the creation of organic content as inbound. Still, in my opinion, if you're attracting someone through advertising, it's considered inbound marketing.

The contrary form of lead generation is outbound, typically referred to as prospecting or, in recruitment, sourcing.

For many companies, job postings are their only form of inbound lead (or candidate) capture.

The biggest challenge with job postings is the ease with which people can apply. You end up with hundreds of applicants, and for many roles, only a tiny percentage of them are truly qualified. This different than inbound lead acquisition in marketing, where the lead quality is much higher - usually greater than 50%.

Sure, not every lead will be qualified, but you can at least expect a percentage of between 50%-80% depending on your market and your messaging.

In recruitment, the number of qualified applicants for some engineering roles is as low as 5%-10%.

Obviously, this varies with the type of role. I've had much higher percentages of qualified candidates who applied to marketing roles I've recruited for in the past.

There could (and should) be questions during this process that force the applicant to confirm if they have the skills and experience listed in the job description's requirements.

If they don't match up, they should automatically be put in a subfolder of applicants to that role and listed as "not qualified."

A nice feature would be an automated email immediately sent thanking them for applying and letting them know they do not meet the requirements. This feature exists in most job boards and ATS platforms. I would recommend using it.

The question then becomes, how do you prevent unqualified people from applying in the first place? How do you encourage them to opt themselves out if it's not for them?

That's a key question and something that should be a core focus of recruitment marketing.

The reality of marketing and life is not everything is for everyone. You actually want people to say to themselves when they come across your job description or company, "this role (or company) is not for me."

That's perfectly fine.

Just as every product or service sold isn't designed for everyone, your roles aren't for everyone. Hell, your company isn't for everyone.

At some point, we became conditioned to think that every product, every service, and therefore every commercial or ad we see should be something we like.

I remember times when I've seen TV commercials that I thought were so stupid. I thought they were garbage and the product they were selling was garbage. I didn't understand why a commercial or product like that even existed. Who would use it?

Now, when I look back, I realize it simply wasn't for me. But it was for someone. Just not me.

Those companies wasted a lot of money showing ads to people who weren't the target market for their product.

I also realize that it's quite fine when people have the same reaction to a product or service I'm marketing, a blog post or podcast I produce, and even jobs that I post.

In fact, I would prefer those people conclude that it's not for them as quickly as possible. More importantly, I need to do a better job of minimizing this from happening in the first place.

Going Beyond Job Postings

I see the role of recruitment marketing going beyond this, which is often the primary form of inbound, to engage with truly passive candidates.

This should be done by a combination of permission marketing (this includes email marketing), social (both paid social and organic social), community building, creating a following around in-company thought leadership, and remarketing, among other things.

Digital marketing is more than Google Ads and social media. It's an ecosystem of touchpoints and communication. It forms a cohesive digital platform telling your story and connecting with those you're for.

II

Part Two

7

Moving Beyond the Old-School Mentality

Wasting the Work

So much work and effort are wasted by recruiters every day. If you were to add it up over the course of a year, the number of people that recruiters engaged and interacted with would be staggering.

Unfortunately, this is the norm. I'm guilty of it from my recruiting days.

I'm talking about doing all of the work required to find the "perfect" candidate for a role, only to find out they're not interested. Most recruiters move on to the next "perfect" candidate who *is* interested, never reaching back out to this person again.

Recruiting isn't easy. There's much thought that goes into finding the right people to contact about a role. It's more than throwing out a job posting to the world, sitting back, and waiting for the most talented people in your industry to flood your inbox. Hint: that *never* happens.

Keep in mind that every role and industry is different. In some cases, all you really need to do is post a job and go through the applicants. However, for some roles, engineering specifically, job postings have a horrible ROI and can be a waste of time.

Maybe not a total waste, but close.

A recruiter spends a reasonable amount of time creating complex Boolean search strings, trying to think of all the different ways the same skill or experience could be named.

For example, someone could be called a software engineer, a software developer, or a computer scientist – and those are just titles.

They could create a search that returns 2,000 possible matches, adding more terms to their search to narrow the matches because they are up against the clock.

This takes time and a lot of tweaks and adjustments.

Then along comes the "perfect" candidate, and they're not interested.

And the recruiter moves on.

They did the work to find whom they were looking for, and they just walked away because the timing wasn't right.

Why not think of this time as an investment that has both short- and long-term returns?

Will that person help you fill the role your manager and hiring manager wanted to be filled yesterday? Certainly not.

But would they be a tremendous asset to the company in the future?

Will you have more roles like this open at some point down the road?

Are they so good that a role is opened so that they could be hired?

If the answer to *any* of these questions is 'yes' then why in the world would you not stay in touch with them?

Why would you not create a system and take advantage of the automation technology that exists to allow you to stay in touch with this person without doing anything in the future once you have an email sequence created and scheduled?

This kind of nurturing is done by Sales Development Reps (SDRs) at SaaS companies. An SDR may sound like a sales role, but it often rolls up to marketing since it is a lead-generating activity.

The technology to easily (and almost effortlessly) create and maintain regular check-ins and follow up with these candidates has never been better than it is now. It will likely only continue to improve through advancements in AI and machine learning.

The "Numbers Game" vs. The Minimal Viable Audience

The "numbers game" is the name I've used to refer to how some people and organizations view sales and recruiting.

The thinking goes that if you contact enough people, usually hundreds (sometimes more than 100 per day), you'll find a couple of interested people. Sounds familiar, doesn't it?

Doesn't this sound a lot like the way I previously described old school marketing was done?

The thinking goes, if the idea is to get your message in the right place, at the right time, why not increase the odds of that happening at least once by sending the same email to hundreds of people. Maybe even thousands.

It does work. You could get 10 replies back for every 100 people you contact. Keep in mind, not all 10 responses will be positive.

After some time of doing this, the percentages start to normalize. You can begin to estimate, with a decent degree of confidence, how many people you need to email or call each day to "find" enough interested people to achieve your goal- which is likely not your goal.

This is probably your manager's goal because it's also what she needs you to accomplish to keep her job. It's because this is an easy thing to measure, and it's the way things have always been done.

She learned this when she started recruiting, as did you. The cycle continues.

Salespeople need to bring in a certain number of sales each month, just like recruiters need to hire a certain number of people each month. If they don't, they'll both be looking for new jobs.

So, if you're in one of these kinds of roles, you quickly begin to figure out how many people you need at each stage of the process or funnel by working backward and using the percentages that have emerged.

Let's use recruiting as an example. We'll assume the hiring manager wants to interview at least five people to feel confident about their offer and hire.

That means you will have to conduct between 10 and 15 phone interviews, maybe more for a tech role.

To get those 10-15 phone interviews, you will either have to prospect (otherwise known as sourcing) and send cold emails and/or place cold phone calls to around 100-150 people that you've found.

If you rely on people applying to your role, you may have to look through 50-250 resumes, again, depending on the type of position. If you're trying to hire a software engineer at a well-known Fortune 500 company like Google, Facebook, Amazon, or Microsoft, only about 5% or fewer of the people who apply will be qualified for your role.

No joke, I've had a plumber apply to a software engineering role when I was at Microsoft.

The reason for these low numbers is because candidates play the 'numbers game' as well. It's so easy to apply to jobs that many people submit applications to any and every job they feel they could do or would like to do. They think that the more they apply to, the better their chances of getting a callback.

At the end of the day, it all comes down to numbers.

None of this is efficient. This kind of strategy doesn't save time in the long run because you have to weed out the people you misidentified. You have to talk to many unqualified prospects and candidates to get to that one great match.

Often, sales organizations view marketing as a lead engine—a way to lessen their prospecting burden by filling the funnel with "warm" leads.

In these organizations, marketers are often expected to act in the same way. Spam and flood the market with their messaging and brand in hopes that they'll get lucky and bump into the right person at the right time who has a problem they can solve.

Given the strong propensity toward managing numbers in recruiting, I'm not hopeful that recruitment marketing and employer branding will be viewed differently. Adding another broken system to an already broken system will amplify the inefficiencies and potentially have a damaging effect on the brand.

One of my book's objectives is to find a better way by looking at better marketing methods and applying them to recruitment marketing and branding.

It can *always* be better.

Enter the concept of the minimal viable audience.

Your Minimal Viable Audience

The concept of a minimal viable audience could be seen as an opposite approach to the way things are currently done.

What is a minimal viable audience anyway? It's a concept I learned from Seth Godin, and both the terms minimal and viable are essential, not just fluff words.

If we break this out into two things (which it actually is), we would have a "minimal audience" and a "viable audience."

Let's look at the term "viable" and what it means to be a "viable audience." According to the Cambridge Dictionary, viable is defined as:

> Able to work as intended or able to succeed.

So, it's just that- it needs to be an audience that works, that fits what you're marketing.

Meaning, they have a problem, and you have a solution that is worth paying for.

It's really as simple as that. What if you were able to look at your current customer base and identify the key attributes they all have in common. What if those attributes could then be used to build a persona that you could use as a template for finding others just like those you currently *viably* serve and were able to make them aware (and interested) in how you can solve their problem?

What about the "minimal audience" aspect of the equation? What if I told you that it wasn't necessary to compile large lists to play the percentages game?

What if I told you a small, highly-targeted list of 50 or 100 prospective candidates would yield better long-term results than a list of 1,000 candidates?

What if you know your existing customers so well that, without a shadow of a doubt, the people you would be reaching out to all have the same problem and are eager to find a solution?

Do you think your reply rate would be better than a list of 1,000 semi-qualified contacts?

This is precisely where the "spray and pray" method comes up short. Instead of focusing on the minimal viable audience, it focuses on the minimal viability of the maximum audience.

The "spray and pray" mentality is a scorched earth mentality. You're forsaking future opportunities to build relationships and hire people who truly are the best match for the role to fill your open role today.

A minimal viable audience is the opposite of this. It's intentional. It's deliberate. It's strategic.

In the long run, focusing on a minimal viable audience will be a much more stable way to build a business and build your employer brand and increase your company's quality of hire in the future.

Keep in mind, the term minimal will be different for everyone. Every market is different. Every business is different.

The biggest challenge to switching from the "spray and pray" status quo to something more deliberate and focused is the way salespeople and recruiters are measured based on such short periods.

There's an underlying feeling of needing to hit the ground running at 100 mph. That blasting your messaging to large lists feels like you're accomplishing something.

Instead, the results of these efforts end up being a few viable leads and many more non-viable leads you have to vet and turn away. This takes time away from spending valuable time getting to know the pain and problems of those you truly can help and those you seek to serve. In the sense of hiring, those who are looking to make a change in their careers and are exploring if your company offers the best route to that change.

In the time I spent in sales, it also seems like the mentality among those on a sales team is one of the prospective customers serving them instead of seeking to serve their prospects.

That's because the entire focus isn't on the problem and solution but on how to line the salesperson's pockets with commission checks.

This can be similar to a numbers-driven recruiting mentality, which focuses on getting annual bonuses and outranking their internal peers.

If we could find ways to measure what truly matters in building great customer relationships, remarkable customer experience, and genuinely solving problems worth paying for, I believe this focus would shift, and a healthier, more viable company would result. The same measurements apply to candidates and employees.

The (Long) Sales Cycle

When it comes to B2B marketing, some sales cycles can take months, sometimes years.

Not only does this require consistent and persistent follow-up and check-ins by a sales team, but this is where the marketing team can make a huge impact through nurturing.

Why do some sales cycles take so long? There can be various reasons ranging from the cost of implementation to regulations to engineering testing that needs to be done to the number of people involved in the purchasing decision.

Deciding to change jobs is no different. It's a life-changing decision and not one that should be taken lightly. There is always a cost to changing jobs; it may not always be obvious. There may be situations in which other people are involved in the decision-making process: a spouse, children, other family members, especially if relocation is involved.

Someone doesn't go from being completely happy one day to eagerly willing to change companies or roles the next.

However, what frequently happens is recruiters and talent sourcers spend an inordinate amount of time searching for and contacting people they think would be good candidates for their open roles. Some of the people they find would be excellent hires and would almost certainly get an offer.

But too often, the recruiters move on if they don't get a reply from their first email or outreach, or the person replies saying they're not interested *at this time.*

So often, the recruiters move on. Never to reach back out to that person again. Or at least anytime soon.

What if they could get that person to engage and stay connected through various marketing campaigns and long-term check-ins?

Then, in a year or 7 months, after the person has given some substantial thought to making a move and where they would want to go, they reach out to your company directly to inquire about working there?

If they end up joining your company, you likely will have spent zero money on job postings and made one of the highest quality hires in years.

All because you were patient, stayed in touch through thoughtful and strategic engagement.

Just because open roles are treated as a transactional part of a business by a hiring team doesn't mean the people being hired view them the same way.

To a recruiter and their manager, one hire isn't enough. To the person being hired, it's a decision that could affect their life for years to come, not to mention their family.

It's time for companies to become more human with their human resources departments.

Which, in my opinion, is one of the biggest naming oxymorons in business.

The Lure of Speed

As I began interviewing people for this book and performed other research, I noticed a familiar term that keeps popping up: programmatic.

In the digital marketing world, programmatic refers to a type of advertising in which automation is used to buy and sell media.[5]

I just assumed when I saw this term being used in a recruitment marketing sense that it was used in the same way. Instead of display ads, it's a way of distributing job ads or job postings.

As I was digging through the Symphony Talent website, I noticed they were grouping email marketing into what it called "programmatic marketing."

This wasn't very clear to me as a marketer. It seems like the term "programmatic marketing" has a different meaning in recruitment marketing than it does in digital marketing.

In my opinion, this type of thing leads to confusion when recruitment marketers with minimal digital experience are trying to learn the basics of marketing.

I also keep seeing mentions of AI (artificial intelligence) and machine learning used.

As I continued scrolling through the Symphony Talent site, I noticed the following claim:

---

[5] https://www.smartinsights.com/internet-advertising/internet-advertising-targeting/what-is-programmatic-marketing/

"Powered by AI and machine learning, it automatically puts the right messages in front of the right people – guiding them down the recruiting funnel toward conversion quickly, seamlessly, and efficiently."

That makes sense and is something that B2B and B2C marketers use marketing automation platforms to achieve. This seems like it offers very similar functionality.

The biggest hang-up I have is with the part about "guiding them down the recruiting funnel toward conversion *quickly*."

That "quickly" part is what I struggle with. The mindset in recruitment marketing seems to be the same as in recruiting – speed, efficiency, and numbers over being deliberate, patient, quality, and long-term value creation.

Don't get me wrong, marketing is also focused on these same short-term things, but it's also balanced with longer-term strategies depending on the sales cycle's length. For some people changing roles or companies, that sales cycle is measured in years, not months or days.

Even in marketing, especially in B2B marketing, which is similar to recruitment marketing, I think there is a shift underway.

This shift is especially evident through an increased focus on ABM (account-based marketing) and the necessity of a long-term nurturing strategy.

Automation is great – for some things. It can automate administrative activities, increase efficiency, and free up marketers, recruiters, and sales to focus on the things that require more thought or effort.

It can also remove the human element and cause major problems if done incorrectly.

Creating efficiencies, coupled with a great end-user experience with automation, takes time and thoughtful design. It also takes meticulous segmentation that I don't trust AI and machine learning to accomplish properly- at least yet.

Wasted Opportunity

How can I not be excited by the opportunity to help companies get better at recruitment marketing?

But, how can I not be a little disappointed that some of the most obvious things are not being done?

How long has email been around? That's a tricky question. It's been around a lot longer than most people think.

A better question, how long has email been an integral part of our work life? Probably the entire lifetime of those now graduating from college.

But yet, email as a recruitment marketing strategy seems to be overlooked. Not just when it comes to recruitment marketing, but digital marketers need to be reminded of it's effectiveness and ROI constantly.

According to SmashFly's 2020 Recruitment Marketing Benchmark report, 47% of companies with talent networks never send another email beyond their confirmation email.

What?!

Then what are you doing with your "talent networks"?

It's also interesting to note that, in the research I've done, the only type of email communication most companies engage in is sign-ups to receive their latest job openings.

Ugh. If you could see me right now, I'm shaking my head with a look of disgust on my face.

This is the same old tired recruiting crap.

Email is just viewed as another form of "spray and pray."

The idea of a talent network has been around for a very long time. They have been horribly designed and mismanaged the majority of the time.

In 2011, when I was at Microsoft, there was a lot of talk about developing talent networks. I think one existed, but I thought it was a waste of time, so I created a community instead.

As someone actively engaged in learning and keeping their pulse on trends, I will not-so-humbly pat myself on the back here and say that I was ahead of my time with this concept.

Communities are a growing (and successful) trend when it comes to marketing and business.

Back to my story...

I created a gated community on LinkedIn that would allow people interested in working on my team at Microsoft a chance to engage with me (and other recruiters) to ask questions and learn more about the team as they considered and weighed their options.

I actually first did this when I was a contract recruiter at Comcast in 2009.

I felt there needed to be something more human than just an automated email blast letting people know about new job openings.

I hear what you're saying about your talent network strategy. You say, "but it's a *targeted* email based on the job preferences someone had ticked off when they signed up."

It doesn't matter. It's not engaging, and it's only sending out what's important to *you* – a job posting for the role you wanted to fill yesterday.

Don't get me wrong. I'm not saying don't share job openings, but that is only a small part of the content you should be sharing through a 'talent network.'

An enormous opportunity exists in the area of candidate nurturing.

It takes effort and thoughtful design. It also takes time.

When someone opts in to hear from you, by all means, communicate with them. Offer them something of value – to them.

There is no greater reward in marketing than when someone tells you they want to hear from you regularly, and that's essentially what people are telling you they want when they give you their email address and name through a subscription form.

Don't waste the opportunity.

8

Funnels and Touchpoints

Filling the Funnel

For as long as I can remember, "fill the funnel" has been a mantra among recruiting professionals and salespeople alike.

The thought is if you fill the funnel with enough people, you're sure to find a good fit for your [INSERT YOUR ROLE, PRODUCT, OR SERVICE HERE].

It's a sloppy, lazy, and expensive bet to make.

It also creates an awful experience for candidates (or customers).

As I've mentioned continuously throughout this book, this is old school, 20th Century, mass marketing.

Demographics are so Mid-20th Century

Modern marketing, if done thoughtfully and correct, is precise. It's focused. It's targeted. It's not done to appeal to everyone.

The core element of modern marketing is knowing who you're *not* for just as much as knowing who you *are* for.

Creating personas based on demographics is so 1960. That's a tactic of mass marketing.

Psychographics is a critical element in modern marketing. Understanding people and their behavior at a personal level. Incorporating empathy into your marketing.

Understanding what motivates people. Answering questions such as why someone chose the profession they're in? Do they want to change professions? What are their values? What story do they tell themselves about work and their career?

These things can sound like they're granular and isolated to each individual, but they can actually be common among a small group of people.

When someone evaluates your company and open role, they're consciously or subconsciously thinking to themselves, 'people like me work at places like this. Is this company for people like me?'

Recruitment marketing isn't about mass marketing and advertising to the masses. It's not about corralling enough of the right people to eventually hire the very best talent for your company. Whether that's filling a role you have open now or one that will open two years from now.

It's about doing the work of finding the right people and engaging and building relationships with them. Helping them figure out if people like them work at a place like your company and being OK if the answer is no.

In fact, it's better to conclude that you're not for them sooner rather than later. It's cheaper, saves time, and is better for everyone.

Funnels and Touchpoints

When I think about the marketing I do now for a B2B company, I think about our objectives and how complex human behavior can be in our digital world, where most of the information we could ever need is literally at our fingertips.

Comparing products or services is easier now than ever. You can read hundreds of customer reviews when before, you'd be lucky to talk to a handful of people who could tell you about their experience.

I also think about this and how it relates to talent acquisition and hiring.

There is a lot of information available about nearly any company you could be interested in working for. You can see the show they try to put on via Facebook and Instagram.

You can read reviews of current and past employees, even obtain salary information about most roles on sites like GlassDoor.

Funnels

In the marketing world, there seem to be people who believe in the concept of a marketing funnel and those who want to push it to the side, saying it no longer applies.

I'm a funnel guy because I haven't heard, read, or seen anything that would convince me that there is a better way of looking at how people make purchasing decisions.

I'm waiting for that to happen.

Sure, does every person follow the exact flow of the funnel leading up to a purchase? Not at all.

But, it provides a way to better understand the kinds of decisions people are likely to make. Where they land in the funnel also gives marketers a better understanding of what they'll be more responsive to when we cross paths.

As I dive into learning more about recruitment marketing and its execution, I'm particularly interested in how the funnel is viewed and what strategies and tactics exist to attract and engage with folks over time.

The funnel is where branding and direct marketing intersect.

Touchpoints and Engagement

How are prospective candidates being engaged with after becoming aware and possibly interested in keeping tabs on your company and future open roles?

Marketers use email marketing platforms like MailChimp and Constant Contact. More advanced marketing teams use marketing automation platforms like Marketo and Pardot at the enterprise level or Sharpspring (I've used in the past), Act-On (my team currently uses), and HubSpot (I've used in the past).

We also are continually shipping and testing landing pages that we send ad and social clicks to. My design team uses Unbounce to easily create and A/B test pages with specific goals and intent.

One of the questions I have, is how are recruitment marketing teams capturing folks higher in the funnel, straddling the Awareness and Engagement parts? Those who may be interested in learning more and someday could be more serious about looking at open roles and career opportunities.

People aren't always searching for roles during normal business hours, so how could you engage with candidates even when you're recruiters are not working?

Ali Hackett, Director and Co-Founder of the recruitment tech company Meet and Engage, says, "on average, 40% of the chatbot conversations that our clients have orchestrated (with candidates) happen outside of office hours or Saturday or Sunday."

That's significant.

What about personas? Are you developing personas built around the kinds of career paths and opportunities you offer people so you can better align with those candidates who are interested in what you have to offer?

Do you have a persona that helps define the kind of people who *don't* do well at your company? People whose career goals don't align with what you have to offer?

Are you creating content that, drip by drip, continuously builds the positive brand sentiment you expect to grow and nurture for your company?

The employment brand folks should get their attention through events and social media, but it's recruitment marketing's role to bring them home.

That's how I've designed the marketing strategy for the B2B company where I'm the Director of Marketing.

We offer useful content as a way to build trust and subsequently engage through email, social, paid search and display ads, and other touchpoints. All of these things help us stay engaged, top-of-mind, and continuously educate people about our products and, most importantly, the services and value-add that we offer.

Twin Funnels - Moving an Audience and Building an Audience

Content creation and distribution are the cornerstones of modern digital marketing.

During the time I was writing this book, I attended the 2020 MarketingProfs B2B Virtual Forum.

Attending conferences like this and SMX, Inbound, and MozCon, among others, is a tremendous way to generate ideas. I've always found that I come away from these conferences with direct knowledge about the things I've learned, but I'm also able to take the concepts discussed and begin thinking of applying them in different ways. Ways that are unique to my business or, in this case, recruitment marketing. Things the presenters may not have originally intended or discussed, but creative applications unique to me and my business or industry.

It was no different this time around.

As I sat through the presentations, I was constantly thinking about what I'm learning and how it can be applied to the B2B company I currently work for, my own future business endeavors, how it could be applied to someone's career (including my own), and, additionally, how it could be incorporated into recruitment marketing.

That's what I love about marketing. It applies to so many things.

During one of the last presentations of the day, Robert Rose talked about content marketing measurement. As I've mentioned before, the marketing funnel is a useful way of visualizing the customer (or candidate) journey.

It helps to map out the touchpoints, a prospective customer's (or candidate's) intent. This helps you identify the appropriate content and next steps to nurture them through the funnel toward becoming a lead (or applicant).

Robert brought up an interesting way of looking at the funnel from the perspective of a twin funnel – the traditional funnel of moving an audience and layering on a content-related funnel to simultaneously build an audience that, at any time, can cross over to the 'moving' funnel.

Here's the visualization he used:

He discussed the value of building an audience - even if the majority of them never become leads or customers. The value lies in the insight you can gain from them. This helps you better build out personas and segmentation and generate referrals through people who may not become candidates but are there to learn from you.

For this book, that could be recruiters and recruitment marketing professionals at other companies.

He then showed how they could "cross" from the "building an audience" funnel to the "moving an audience" funnel, ultimately becoming a lead (or applicant).

This really piqued my interest, and I see some real cross-over value to how recruitment marketers can think about their content and how it maps to their overall nurturing and content strategy.

9

Focus on Who You're For, Understand Who You're Not For

Competition and Positioning

I've found that there are two camps of people when it comes to marketing. Those who preach competitive analysis, research, and know their competitors almost as much as they know their own company, and those who say competition is irrelevant.

I'm somewhere in the middle.

I *don't* believe that you should obsess about your competition and change your core values or attributes as a reaction to what they do.

I *do* believe you should understand what other options exist in the market and how you fit into it and are perceived.

When looking for another role, people (depending on where they live) could have many different options.

Having an understanding of each company you could be competing against would be overkill. But understanding the mix of companies could help you recognize where you fit into the mix and how you want to stand out from those you're for. This also means making it clear for those you're not for.

The possibilities are endless when it comes to the kinds of companies you could choose. For some people, the status of working for a well-known Fortune 100 company is what they seek. For others, it's the diversity of what you can work on and the ability to influence outcomes, which may be more accessible at a smaller company.

If you're a Fortune 100 company, how are you different from other large companies with similar roles?

When I was a recruiter at Microsoft, I understood what I was up against when I found out a candidate was also interviewing with Google, Facebook, and Amazon.

At the time, Facebook had recently gone public (2012), and people saw the money flying around. They wanted to be a part of that. They also didn't have the negative reputation they have now.

Google offered people something called "20 percent time," which meant you could use 20% of your time on any Google-related passion project.

I was recruiting software engineers at the time, and this is a desirable perk for people whose core passion is to build things.

Amazon's stock was going through the roof, and they would dangle stock options like a carrot at the end of a stick. Their base salaries and bonus program were meager compared to other companies in the big tech space, but some people sought this kind of payoff over time and betting that the stock growth would remain strong.

Amazon knew this and worked people very hard. I knew that I could probably get people to make a switch if they had only been there six months or less. At that time, they would have realized what they had gotten themselves into, and none of their stock options had vested at that point, so they wanted out. This was several years ago, and the environment at Amazon has likely changed - especially in light of a scathing New York Times article published in 2015.

Microsoft's position as an employer in this market was more around work-life balance. Which after leaving, I will say it is relative to the market and industry. I wouldn't call what I had at Microsoft a good work-life balance compared to what I have now working for a smaller company where I can count on one hand the number of emails I've received over a weekend. There is only one time in the five years I've worked there that I was asked to do something over the weekend.

This also applies to smaller companies competing against these giants. You likely can't compete with the shiny perks that are dangled in front of people by the tech giants and some startups – which, by the way, are really designed to keep people at the office for more extended periods.

But you can compete on many other levels.

When I worked at Booking.com, they didn't hide the fact that they weren't very competitive when it came to the salaries they offered, but they were very clear about being a great place to work for people who loved travel. I feel that their strategy has worked as far as employee attraction and retention. I don't have any facts or figures around this other than what I've noticed through my connections at the company, and there are many people that I knew when

I worked with them who are still there nearly five years later.[6]

I say all of this because knowing where you fit in will help you craft and deliver messaging that will attract the people you *are* for, dissuade those you're not for, which saves time and is a good long-term strategy.

There is nothing wrong with making it clear who you are and who you're for. There's something very wrong about being a marketer and not knowing these things.

Purpose and Values

Purpose and values are becoming more important to people, not only around what they buy but also where they work.

I believe this will be even more prevalent in the wake of everything that happened in 2020 due to COVID-19, social unrest, and nasty election-year politics.

People are taking stock of what's most important to them. They may have to settle for having a 'job' until the economy rebounds but will not be so willing to settle on the next career-related role they take.

People will have stronger values coming out of the crises of 2020, and I believe more people will be seeking work that has purpose.

---

[6] Since writing this, COVID-19 has devastated the travel industry and many companies have been forced to lay off employees. As a result, some of the people I worked with are no longer there but this wasn't by their own choice. In reading the positive feedback from those affected, Booking.com was able to maintain trust and respect among those employees laid off because of the way they handled it with empathy and grace.

Companies that can promote and live up to their promise of a clear purpose will reap tremendous benefits in attracting and retaining the best employees.

This can be a remarkable competitive advantage in a multitude of ways. Not just in attracting and retaining the best talent in your market, but in attracting and retaining customers. After all, that's what pays the employees' salaries, and without customers, you have no business. Many companies, such as Southwest Airlines, have proven that happy employees result in happy customers.

In fact, when Southwest hires new employees, they're less interested in someone's skills and more focused on three key attributes, or intangible skills, that have more impact on their customers. They refer to these three attributes as a warrior spirit, a servant's heart, and a fun-loving attitude.[7]

If done well, it's also something that can easily vault you ahead of your competition because most companies fail at effectively articulating their purpose and values.

According to a study done by Strategy& in which they surveyed 540 participants across a wide range of industries, they found that only 22% of the employees agreed that their job allows them to leverage their strengths and skills fully. Only 28% felt fully connected to the company's purpose.[8]

Having a clear purpose also inspires people. The information below shows how employees feel (passionate, excited, motivated, satisfied, and proud) at companies that can clearly present their purpose and the value this creates for customers compared to companies that have not clearly articulated their

---

[7] *How Southwest Airlines Hires Such Dedicated People*, Harvard Business Review - https://hbr.org/2015/12/how-southwest-airlines-hires-such-dedicated-people

[8] https://www.strategyand.pwc.com/gx/en/unique-solutions/capabilities-driven-strategy/approach/research-motivation.html

purpose.

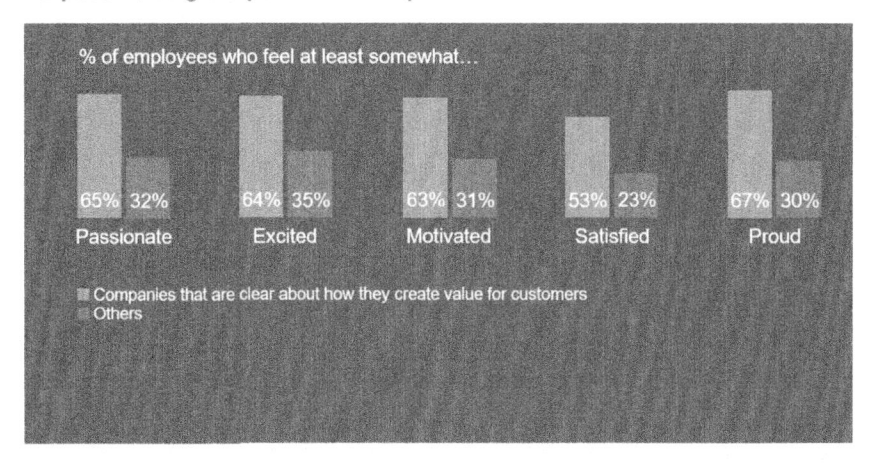

Purpose holds great potential to inspire

% of employees who feel at least somewhat...

Passionate	Excited	Motivated	Satisfied	Proud
65% / 32%	64% / 35%	63% / 31%	53% / 23%	67% / 30%

■ Companies that are clear about how they create value for customers
■ Others

Source: Strategy&

As a marketer, especially when it comes to recruitment and employer branding, it is critical to articulate your company's purpose clearly and, most importantly, provide proof that you're able to live up to what you say.

One way to understand if your organization has a clear purpose is to ask employees who are several layers away from the C-Suite to clearly define how your company adds unique value to its customers.[9]

If they can accurately and easily describe this, ask them if they would be willing to provide you with a quote or testimonial that can be used in your recruitment marketing and employer branding messaging, content, and communication.

---

[9] https://hbr.org/amp/2019/11/why-are-we-here

Testimonials and social proof are among the best ways to quickly build trust and inclusion when marketing to people who are top-of-funnel.

Values

People's worldviews will undoubtedly change following the COVID-19 pandemic in 2020.

I believe many of us will evaluate every aspect of our lives, including our jobs and careers, and make an intentional and conscious effort to better align with how we spend our time and energy-related to our values.

This change will leave some companies in the rear-view mirror when it comes to hiring and employee retention.

I hope that the emphasis will move away from their singular focus on shareholders to a more intentional focus on customers and employees. I hope companies will finally realize that these two components ultimately result in long-term profitability and resiliency compared to the short-term, knee-jerk focus on shareholders getting paid each quarter.

I also hope that people will move away from joining or building startups through the rose-colored 'get rich quick' lens to more of a lens of contribution for the good of their communities, society as a whole, and long-term viability.

It will take a cataclysmic force to spur such change, and I think that moment has arrived.

I know it has for me. When I think about the remainder of my career, it now looks a lot different than it did only six months before writing this book.

What's important to me maybe hasn't changed, but my focus on it has.

My values have become stronger and more focused, and I want to ensure that the work I do every day is focused on making the world better in some way. If I can improve the candidate experience at just one company, I will have helped candidates maintain dignity and a sense of self-worth that can sometimes be broken down through the job-seeking and interviewing process.

I may not contribute to world peace or the environment in a major way, but I can help a few people feel better about themselves, and that kind of impact adds up over time.

10

Internal Marketing

Retention Rate and Replacement Costs

Another thing that is often overlooked, at least as a marketing function, is customer retention and advocacy.

A similar HR function is employee retention through training and a focus on employee mobility. Happy employees with a sense of purpose and future are a valuable asset to recruitment marketing because they will become an advocate for working at the company. This will generate high-quality referrals, which can be a remarkable competitive advantage when hiring.

It's often more powerful when employees promote the work environment and growth opportunities available at their company than when someone in recruitment, HR, or marketing does the same.

If you think about how many employees voluntarily leave their roles and why, not only are companies losing money to replace those employees, but they're losing an opportunity to make it cheaper to hire future employees through employee referrals and positive public sentiment.

In 2019, the average monthly employee turnover rate in the U.S. was 3.2%.[10]

According to a Work Institute study, nearly 22% of those leaving left for better career development, and 12% left for better work-life balance. Only 9% left because of compensation.[11]

This is significant because, at a conservative cost of $15,000 per lost employee, it cost companies an estimated $475 billion from departure factors controllable by the employers.

These costs include things like recruiter fees, temporary replacement workers, and lost productivity.[12]

As companies grow, they are spending money to replace those that left and hiring for new roles as the result of company growth.

That adds up to high costs. Costs could be cut dramatically by focusing on providing more opportunities to develop and grow existing employees and improving their happiness and willingness to promote the company as an employer.

Yet, so few companies invest in this. It's maddening and doesn't make sense.

---

[10] **Source: *The ADP Research Institute® 2019 State of the Workforce Report: Pay, Promotions and Retention***

https://www.adp.com/resources/articles-and-insights/adp-research-institute/research-topics/-/media/62FB03253C3B4B80A2EE73EB8EC29B82.ashx

[11] **Source: Work Institute's *2019 Retention Report***

https://info.workinstitute.com/hubfs/2019%20Retention%20Report/Work%20Institute%202019%20Retention%20Report%20final-1.pdf)

[12] **Source: *To Have and to Hold*; Theresa Agovino;**
https://www.shrm.org/hr-today/news/all-things-work/pages/to-have-and-to-hold.aspx

Training, Learning, and Employee Retention

Just as customer retention is often the responsibility of marketing and sales, employee retention should be viewed similarly.

For the most part, I would assert that most professionals want to learn and continue to grow in their roles.

As a recruiter, I used to hear this frequently. The lack of learning and career growth opportunities within a company were usually the primary reasons someone wanted to leave their current company. Money often was seldom brought up as a primary reason.

Unfortunately for most, they are likely to find that the grass isn't usually greener. Usually, it's the same shade of green at a new company.

Especially given that according to a Gartner survey, 70% of employees feel they haven't mastered the skills they need for their current roles.[13]

That's staggering!

When a new hire joins a company, they're usually eager to dig in and learn. They want to learn and grow, but yet so few are allowed to do so.

When it comes to training and ongoing education, many companies only provide the bare minimum, and it shows in the research surveys being done.

The training they receive covers things like the company's sexual harassment policy and other HR-related topics and how to use their sometimes

---

[13] https://www.gartner.com/en/human-resources/trends/reskilling-the-workforce-infographic

proprietary, antiquated technology.

But, after that, the employees are usually on their own.

If they do employ a training program, it's usually a one-size-fits-all-drinking-from-a-firehose class. Or they encourage the stockpiling of learning credits. Failing to focus on what's truly important to the individual employee to do their current role, not to mention advance their skills.

Training and employee education are most effectively done in small chunks over time as the employee needs it and in a way that helps them push the boundaries of what they know as well as their comfort zone.

There has always been a lot of talk about employees being a company's greatest asset or investment, yet the actions don't reflect this.

III

Part Three

11

Focusing on the Wrong Things

Spray and Pray Doesn't Work

The old model of casting the widest net you can and spend your valuable time sorting through the noise to find that one oyster with the pearl no longer works. It no longer works because it doesn't have to.

In the early, pre-internet days of marketing, the name of the game was mass marketing. The company with the biggest budget won because they could obtain the widest reach and play the odds of getting in front of the right people simply by sheer volume.

Now, specific targeting is the name of the game. If you're going for reach, it can be much more targeted now.

However, not everyone views the internet this way. They see it as a new way of casting that wide net, only it provides a bigger net. You can easily reach many people for a relatively low cost compared to what it took to do the same through traditional marketing.

People took this old-school of mass marketing and leveraged the power of digital to amplify their message, only creating a vast sea of noise and distractions in the process.

This "spray and pray" approach no longer works. I'm not sure if it ever really was a successful strategy, at least an efficient and economical one.

The ability to have unprecedented reach at unprecedented low costs is attractive and comes with the feeling of a leveled playing field for smaller companies.

That's the contradiction of digital.

The real value exists in your ability to be hyper-focused and hyper-targeted with who receives your message.

Being for the few and only ensuring your message gets in front of them is the real benefit of the current digital landscape.

Using technology to specifically target, attract, nurture, and cultivate, and eventually convince the right person to take action is where you should be focusing your time, effort, and budget.

Just because you *can* reach everyone doesn't mean you should.

The ability to isolate and target your ideal audience keeps getting easier every year.

Through paid social, which is advertising on social sites like LinkedIn and Facebook, you have the ability to upload email lists and market to them via ads in their feeds. You can also take those lists one step further and create lookalike audiences, which are essentially audiences that look just like the one you uploaded, and you can get your message in front of them as well.

Market research has never been easier thanks to a new tool on the market called SparkToro.

SparkToro helps you identify where your target market is engaged the most online and get your ads in front of them there. You can find out what podcasts they listen to, what social media accounts they follow and engage with the most and a host of other important information.

It helps take your ad placement and influencer program to the next level.

Recruiting is Essentially a Sales Role

My experience is diverse. In addition to loads of recruitment and digital marketing experience, I also have quite a bit of sales experience.

I've been a prospector and a closer, so I've been involved with outbound and inbound sales.

Having had this experience in sales, including at a SaaS company, I can say that recruiting is a form of sales. At the very least, I can confidently say it's much closer to being a sales role than a marketing role.

Today, many sales teams (especially at SaaS companies) consist of three kinds of roles: SDRs (sales development reps), Account Managers or Account Executives, and Customer Success.

Larger companies have recreated this same model with their recruiting team. I experienced this when I was a recruiter at Microsoft.

Let's break down what these roles do and how they are similar to recruiting roles.

SDRs are the 'hunters' and prospectors. Very similar to the Talent Sourcer role at most large companies. Account Managers are the 'closers,' much like the Recruiters (known as Staffing Consultants at Microsoft).

Where I couldn't find a direct correlation between sales teams and recruiting teams was the Customer Success role. If I had to point to an HR role for this, it would be around employee retention and growth. Which, sadly, few companies invest in these days.

I'm currently building an outbound sales program at my current company, and I'm thinking about the skills and experience needed to be successful in an SDR role.

After giving it much thought, I'll be targeting someone who is currently in a Talent Sourcer role and may be looking for a career change into more of a business role.

An SDR's primary role is to take a persona built by the marketing team, find people who match it and work at companies that use our products. They create a list of these folks, develop messaging (that they'll continuously test), and send cold emails.

This is essentially the same thing a Talent Sourcer does in their role, and they're damn good at it. Likely better than most people currently in a sales role.

When I explained this to the President of our company, he was intrigued at first and then became all in on the idea after thinking about it more.

It's also prevalent for SDRs to report and roll up to marketing because they're engaged in a lead generation activity. That's essentially the role of marketing - lead gen.

Since this SDR role will report to me in marketing, they would have significant exposure to digital marketing. It would be a tremendous learning opportunity for anyone looking to pivot out of recruiting. I'm excited to hire someone and see if my hypothesis comes true.

However, a sales team of Account Managers can't solely rely on outbound leads. There also needs to be a steady stream of inbound leads, which is what my marketing team produces: targeted, qualified inbound leads.

Inbound leads are generated from many different marketing activities, including paid search (Google Ads), paid social, social, SEO, and organic site traffic, content, and nurturing through email marketing.

I found diverse inbound programs weren't being fully utilized, and nurturing programs were non-existent as my marketing experience began to grow toward the end of my time in recruiting.

In outbound programs, SDRs do a lot of nurturing through email. Recruiting is a little more nuanced from sales in that it takes more time to identify and qualify candidates.

Given this, I don't think sourcers should be given the added responsibility of nurturing candidates. This would be better served as a separate role. There are too many moving parts when it comes to executing an effective nurturing program.

Technology would also play a huge role in a candidate nurturing program.

The Role of Technology in Recruiting

Over the course of writing this book, I've been able to have conversations with quite a few people who are doing some exciting things in HR Tech, especially around improving engagement, follow up, and the candidate experience.

This is long overdue.

The candidate experience on many employer websites is still horrible – clunky, time-consuming, and not mobile-friendly. Many designs don't take into account that someone may be interested in a role at your company and are not in a position to apply when they're on your site.

Employers are spending a lot of time and money on social media and interrupting your scroll.

The challenge with this is that most people engage with social media on their phones. Your candidate experience must take this into account and optimize for mobile.

A large population of people isn't quite ready to change jobs or companies. Still, they are interested in learning more about the opportunities, culture, and other aspects of working at other companies.

This is where a well-thought strategy around nurturing and engagement will pay dividends in the future. To do this manually at scale would be nearly impossible for most companies, and that is why it often doesn't currently happen.

Things like chatbots, live chat events, and marketing automation are essential elements of creating an engaging experience for candidates and improving a recruiting team's efficiency and productivity.

When introducing automation into a system, the design is critical. Time must be spent thinking and analyzing each touchpoint involved and how they will be viewed from the candidate's perspective.

12

Where Do I Start?

Where to Start

Start slow. It doesn't have to be all-in. Be deliberate and intentional about your focus and objectives- especially your long-term objectives. Understand your gaps and what needs to be learned, hired, or outsourced.

It's OK to outsource resources at first, as you build and refine processes and your strategy.

It may also be that some things are more manual at first, and that's perfectly fine. In fact, I would recommend it. It would be best if you nailed the basics before you can automate.

The Lure of Automation

Who doesn't love automation and being able to free up your time from administrative and repetitive tasks?

Automation is the main selling point of a lot of tools and platforms right now.

Which is great. If you know what you're doing.

If you don't know what you're doing, automation will only compound it. It will shine a spotlight on it.

If you're building a recruitment marketing program, think to yourself, "what's the most impactful thing I should focus on first?" but also consider, "what's one of the things I should be doing that will take the most time to build and gain momentum?"

Starting with a mix of easy wins and smaller projects will get things moving and build momentum. This will also help you identify gaps and things to be tightened up.

The larger things will obviously require more time, so the sooner you can get those projects moving, the better.

Enter, Email Marketing

When you think about the two questions I've recommended you ask yourself, a great place to start answering both questions is email marketing.

At the heart of email marketing is audience building and permission marketing.

Email still works. When done right, it can be highly targeted and can deliver, by far, the biggest ROI of any of your marketing activities.

But like everything else in life that's good, it takes time to build and gain momentum.

Hire someone with email marketing experience. You want to get this right. Putting someone in charge of email marketing that doesn't know how to segment and manage audience lists will only create a giant mess.

(I will go into more detail about building an email marketing program later in this book, for now, keep it top of mind.)

Timing, messaging, and measurement are critical elements of a successful email marketing strategy. Hiring someone with this experience will set you up for long-term success- even if they're a contract freelancer or agency.

You can start with a simple email marketing platform like Emma, AWeber, or MailChimp.

These are 'simple' platforms with advanced automation and sequencing capabilities that can immediately be utilized by someone who knows what they're doing.

Don't be tempted to go too big right away unless you hire a very experienced email marketing professional who understands the candidate journey right out of the gate. That's probably unlikely. There will be a learning curve involved when it comes to your audience.

Because I think this is so important, I'll mention it again - you'd be better off hiring someone who knows what they're doing, letting them build the foundation. This means not promoting a recruiter into this role.

It's also a good idea to identify one target segment or audience you want to focus on first. It may be tempting to build your email program around all of the evergreen roles you're always hiring for, but that will only complicate things and may actually increase the amount of time it takes to build the program and get it up and running initially.

Start small. Test, refine, and test some more. This is easiest when you limit the number of variables involved.

As you begin doing the necessary testing, it's key to understand your audience, including their psychographic profile. An experienced email marketer will want to do this.

THEN, and only then, you can begin to identify areas to automate. Slowly. It's not a race.

Stop thinking about marketing from a quarterly or monthly perspective. Think about it from a momentum-building, long-term perspective, with short-term wins sprinkled in.

Nothing great was accomplished the first time it was tried.

Slow. Deliberate. Focused.

That's the name of the game. But, a point of emphasis on not getting hung up on perfect. There's a difference between being deliberate and focused and being perfect.

It will never be perfect. Get it out into the world to be tested, but be deliberate and focused on how you do this.

This is how success and true competitive advantages are achieved.

You Already Have a Recruitment Marketing Team; You Just Don't Know It

Most companies already have the expertise needed; it's just siloed and unable to be accessed due to corporate structures and politics.

A company doesn't need a recruitment marketing team when they already have a marketing team. They certainly shouldn't try converting a junior recruiter into a marketing Swiss Army Knife.

That's doomed to failure because marketing is more than being on social media.

When it comes to large corporate enterprises, maybe it makes sense to create a holistic team focused solely on recruitment marketing. But, for growing SMB's who already have a well-designed marketing team in place, what you really need is someone in a director-level role responsible for driving your recruitment marketing.

You already have content writers, email marketers, social media specialists, an advertising team, and SEO specialists. You have people who are comfortable and proficient in the use of analytics platforms like Google Analytics.

Take advantage of that. There's no need to duplicate skills or hire an outside agency to do what you're already capable of doing.

The key lies in tying the two teams – recruitment and marketing – together through strategic leadership and direction.

Someone with one foot in both teams. They're essentially a technical program manager, a liaison who can speak the language of marketing and recruitment, translating requirements and objectives between the two groups.

This person would work side-by-side with their peers in marketing and talent acquisition.

Recruitment marketing would be woven into the fabric of their overall marketing strategy.

Start Small and Collaborate

I know what you're asking…what about the budget? As the leader of Talent Acquisition, you would likely own that. You'll just have to come up with a way of tracking it cross-functionally.

After all, you're all part of the same company. Stop acting like individual businesses with different goals. You all are pushing toward the same thing.

I've described a situation in which your in-house marketing team acts as an agency for Talent Acquisition.

Is it impossible? Not at all. Is it difficult? Probably. But that's why they hired you and the marketing leaders- to solve problems, do the difficult work, and create a competitive advantage that will continue to propel the company forward.

As I mentioned earlier, being able to leverage your company's already-existing marketing resources will be key. I've also described the kind of person that would be ideal to lead your recruitment marketing initiative.

This person could essentially be a "team of one" as someone in a strategic program manager role and a hybrid of a director and someone 'in the weeds' getting their hands dirty with some of the tactical work.

However, I would highly recommend starting with a team of two – a program manager/director and someone with email marketing, permission marketing, and lead nurturing experience.

This would include experience with platforms like MailChimp, Emma, or AWeber (all you would need at first). Marketing automation experience would be important because you will likely graduate from an email-only platform to a marketing automation platform as you begin to scale and develop your candidate nurturing program at scale.

However, if you don't have much experience with email marketing and candidate nurturing, you may not fully understand all of the functionality that comes with a complex marketing automation platform, and you will essentially have a costly email marketing platform on your hands.

Suppose you can find someone in the program manager/director role that has hands-on experience with that, great. However, this could take up a significant amount of his or her time, which would detract from the important work of developing strategy, working across marketing and recruitment, and analysis.

A great candidate profile for this role would be someone who comes from a digital marketing agency background. Specifically, someone who has been an Account Director or Account Manager at a full-service agency. Full-service means the agency offered everything – email marketing, SEO, paid media, analytics, you name it. Some agencies only focus on one area, like paid media.

The Program Manager (or Director) would develop the strategy and work cross-functionally as a bridge between recruitment and marketing. They would work with you to manage the recruitment marketing budget and collaborate with the marketing team.

They would ensure a smooth transition between the recruiters (or sourcers if you have them) and recruitment marketing to capture candidates to be put into the nurture funnel.

This person would manage the advertising and work with external vendors on this along with other outsourced elements.

They would build the nurturing and permission marketing program and oversee the person who manages and executes this.

They would develop campaigns, including social media, and work with the marketing team and other resources to execute against them.

Human-Centered Design

If you've reached this chapter of the book, you undoubtedly understand the importance of empathy and have a deep understanding of your target audience at a human level.

For all of the efficiencies and benefits that come along with technology, AI, and automation, if they aren't done with human interaction in mind, they will fail miserably.

The thing about automation and AI is that humans design them. Everything from the look and feel of the product, how it interacts with people, to what words are used.

This is a tremendous opportunity to get it right and utilize the technology in its intended ways.

If you were to ask a group of recruiters if they've ever applied to a job using their company's technology, I would guess the majority would say no.

It can be a cumbersome and bad experience in many instances, and the recruiters generally are unaware of how bad it is.

When implementing new technology like a CRM or marketing automation platform, take the time to understand exactly how it works at every candidate touchpoint. Do everything you can to understand the candidate, their needs and wants, and what they are genuinely interested in and seeking at every communication stage you could have with them.

Understand what action they will most likely want to take and provide that opportunity for them. Use the technology from a user's perspective and engage in user-acceptance testing.

A great book on this topic that I would highly recommend is *Rocket Surgery Made Easy* by Steve Krug. The book's basis is about testing website design, but the core principles can be applied to nearly anything.

When looking back on the early days of my marketing career, there was a time that I thought every marketing touchpoint created an opportunity for lead generation.

I would recommend that my design team put lead-gen CTA's on every landing page we created. Things like "Request a Quote" or "Request More Info" with a form to capture their name, email, and sometimes more, depending on the value of the offer we were making.

We gated, not just our most valuable content, but most of our less valuable content as well.

Later, as I was developing our lead nurturing program, I wanted to understand our site visitors better. So, I began to think more about what they were doing when they clicked on our ad. What was their intent? What did they expect to see after they clicked the ad? Then, it dawned on me that we were missing out on a huge opportunity.

The opportunity wasn't a way to generate more leads; it provided more value to our site visitors (and potential future customers) and began to build trust and brand recognition.

The company I work for is a B2B company, and we market primarily to engineers. The sales cycle is long and often starts with the design and building of prototypes. A lot of testing is before any orders of meaningful volumes are placed. The payoff to all of this is once our products are chosen, they are usually 'spec'd in,' which essentially means they're locked into the design. If the company wanted to change vendors, they would need to go through another exhaustive round of component testing.

Through this exercise, I realized that if an engineer clicked on one of our display ads or paid social ads, they weren't in 'buy' mode. Our ad had interrupted their day but piqued their interest. It may have spoken to a problem they have or a product they're designing.

Most of the time, they aren't ready to engage with a salesperson or may not even know the specifications of the products they need. But they are interested in taking some collateral with them. Similar to how people walk around the showroom floor at a tradeshow: browsing, getting ideas, and collecting information.

I decided to remove the forms from all of the landing pages our display and paid social ads pointed to and, instead, provide ungated, downloadable product or service one-sheets or other useful collateral. This one-sheet would be branded and include a link to our website and a trackable phone number to measure calls as an offline lead.

The results were astounding. Phone calls increased, specifically from our one-sheet collateral. It also allowed us to use display and social retargeting ads to stay top-of-mind as they progressed down their buying journey.

By shifting my focus from a lead gen-first, inward-focused mindset to something more human- and customer-focused, it made all the difference.

If you focus on helping people solve problems at every step of their journey, it will pay huge dividends in the future.

Instead of asking us for more information through completing a form or engaging with an automated chatbot, we provided what they would need at that very moment and made it easy for them.

This is a critical mindset to have when implementing automation and AI.

What problem are you helping the end-user solve?

Are they happy in their current role but realize it may be time to move on in a year or two?

Is the economy in the tank, and does the person feel secure in their current role but is unhappy?

Maybe they're willing to 'tough it out' for another year or so. Still, when the economy begins to recover, and they feel more inclined to accept the risk of changing roles and companies, they'll act and begin to engage with your content, ultimately applying to an open role.

If you were in their shoes, what kind of experience would you want and expect?

What information would you be interested in?

What level of communication would you expect?

13

Own Your Audience, Don't Rent It

Four Reasons to Get Back to the Basics of Permission Marketing

Shifting your focus from rented audiences on social media to owned audiences through permission marketing will level up your recruitment marketing.

Over the course of writing this book, I've had many conversations with recruitment marketing and employer brand folks. One consistent thread has been how reliant they are on social media and how little they focus on permission and email marketing.

Here are four reasons why you shouldn't put all of your employer brand and recruitment marketing eggs in one basket with social media.

1. Algorithms Change

Social networks are constantly evolving, testing, and changing their algorithms to ensure you engage more and stay on their platform longer.

Most don't share these changes with their users, so it's a guessing game about what you can do to increase your content's reach and engagement.

LinkedIn is the exception, and you can find a wealth of information by reading their engineering blog. [14]

They recently published an article on the importance of 'dwell time' as a key measure of engagement.[15] Given this, dwell time may be the most important measure determining whether your content gains traction among your network or finds the relaxing but frustrating chirp of crickets.[16]

If you manage your brand's social media and haven't read this yet, I'd highly recommend it.

If you're still operating under the assumption that clicks, likes, and shares are the most important things to measure, you may be wondering why those things have dropped off over time.

What does this mean? It means less control of when your message lands and who sees it. You're at the mercy of a machine determining the relevancy and importance of your content and message.

2. Targeting and Segmentation

When it comes to social media, anyone can follow you. You could argue that anyone could also subscribe to your email list from your website, and you wouldn't be wrong. The difference is you have control of how you segment your subscribers on the backend. Just because they subscribed doesn't mean

---

[14] **LinkedIn Engineering Blog- https://engineering.linkedin.com/blog**

[15] https://engineering.linkedin.com/blog/2020/understanding-feed-dwell-time

[16] *Understanding Dwell Time to Improve LinkedIn Feed Ranking*
    - https://engineering.linkedin.com/blog/2020/understanding-feed-dwell-time

you only have one list and email everyone the same message.

Segmentation is a huge advantage of email marketing. You can also invite people to subscribe, essentially 'hand-picking' the people you want to receive your messages.

With social media, you could have 1,000 followers, and maybe only half of them are ones you want to engage with and stay top of mind. Because organic social reach is so low (more on that later), your message will only be seen by a small percentage at any given time, so the likelihood of it getting in front of the ones you want to see it are slim.

This isn't much different from the engagement you would get by placing a display ad (aka banner ad) on websites through Google Ads or another platform. At least engagement as it relates to a display ad means clicks through to your website. That's usually not the case with social network engagement. More on that later, as well.

3. Low Organic Reach (aka "Pay to Play")

This is the big one. Organic reach on social media platforms has been decreasing, little by little, each year since around 2012.

The most recent stats I've seen on organic Facebook reach was about 5.2%.[17] That means, if you have 1,000 followers, only 50 will ever see your organic post at any given time. 5-0.

That's it.

With email, even if people delete your email without opening it, they've seen your brand. The average open rate for email marketing campaigns is close

---

[17] https://blog.hootsuite.com/organic-reach-declining/

to 18%, and the average CTR (click-through rate) is about 2.6%.[18] You'd be lucky to get that from a paid social campaign.

I've also seen a disturbing trend pointing to an inverse relationship between your number of followers and organic reach.

According to a Hootsuite study of Facebook, there was an inverse relationship between the number of fans your page has and the engagement rate. The average engagement rate for pages with less than 10,000 fans was 0.52% compared to 0.28% for pages with between 10,000 and 100,000 fans and 0.10% for pages with more than 100,000 fans.[19]

Essentially, what this means is even if you want to reach the people who have opted-in and want to hear from you, you're going to have to pay. Social media is just another form of paid advertising.

4. Competing Priorities

Often, your goal of using social platforms as a distribution channel to drive traffic to your website directly competes with the platform's goal of keeping you within its walls.

As I mentioned, driving traffic to your website through organic reach is wishful thinking. Most social media platforms want your eyeballs to stay right where they are – on their platform. They want you to scroll, pause, scroll, pause. If you leave, it's because you clicked on a paid post, and they got paid.

As I previously mentioned, part of LinkedIn's algorithm measures the amount

---

[18] https://www.campaignmonitor.com/resources/guides/email-marketing-benchmarks/

[19] https://www.slideshare.net/DataReportal/digital-2020-october-global-statshot-report-october-2020-v01

of time you pause (aka dwell time). They want to reward the people who can help them lengthen the time people stay engaged on their platform.

If you've watched the Netflix documentary *The Social Dilemma*, you saw how these platforms are engineered around our psychology. They're essentially hijacking our minds and bodies for *their* benefit, not that of ourselves or our businesses.

What Else Should You Be Doing?

Don't get me wrong. I'm not saying to stop using social media. I'm saying that if you're mostly focusing on social media, you should reconsider your strategy.

Modern marketing is omnichannel marketing- meaning the way people consume and gather information contains multiple touchpoints.

Viewing social as one of many touchpoints is a good way of looking at it. Still, the most underrated and underappreciated marketing strategies are permission marketing and email marketing.

By building lists that can be segmented and targeted based on your business objectives, you will be taking advantage of your *owned* audience.

When you *rent* your audience on social, you're mostly hoping for a positive outcome. Stop hoping.

Continue to leverage organic social, carve out a budget for paid social campaigns, and focus on ways to increase your reach and targeting through permission marketing. Ultimately, having segmented lists that you own not only will ensure your messages get in front of the right people, but it also offers a substantial competitive advantage.

Permission Marketing: The Undisputed and Still Undefeated Champion of Modern Marketing

Permission marketing has been around for quite a while. Seth Godin wrote a book about it back in 1999.

The thing about permission marketing is that its importance will continue to grow, even if the way you communicate changes.

As digital marketing has gained traction over the past 20-plus years, mass marketing (or some form of it) has only become more accessible.

Anyone can create a display ad and get it in front of hundreds of thousands of people within hours at a relatively low cost.

There are innumerably more ways to grab our attention now than there were 20 years or even 5 years ago.

Social media is one of those attention-grabbing channels. It ushered in the ability to reach thousands of people for free and say whatever you wanted.

Now that's throttled by an algorithm, and it's moved toward a pay-to-play business model.

People ignore display ads. Reaching the people who have seemingly raised their hands and want to hear from you on social now costs money.

The one tried and true pillar of permission marketing remains email.

That doesn't mean it's the only way to communicate with people.

There's also social messaging, text messages, and a host of other means.

The point being, when someone gives you their permission to communicate with them, you should treat that like gold.

The expectations around what they are interested in receiving from you and what you deliver should be crystal clear and shouldn't be deviated from.

In our age of non-stop distractions and ever-increasing competition for our attention, permission marketing remains the most effective marketing channel around. Don't blow it. As Eminem said in his song "Lose Yourself":

If you had
  One shot
  Or one opportunity
  To seize everything you ever wanted
  In one moment
  Would you capture it?
  Or just let it slip?

Someone's permission is the greatest asset a modern marketer could have.

Don't let it slip. Seize the opportunity.

Email Marketing – Still Overlooked and Still Effective

My morning run was spent thinking about the most significant need organizations have when it comes to recruitment marketing. I then thought about how the things I work with every day as a Director of Marketing (mostly digital marketing) correlate to hiring people.

Some of the channels include: email, social, paid media (paid search, paid social, and display), content (blogs, downloadable resources, videos), and search engine optimization (SEO).

From what I've seen of recruitment marketing and employer branding, I would assert that organizations are probably doing pretty well at social and, possibly, content. But beyond that, I haven't seen examples of any of the other channels being used consistently.

You may be surprised to know that, even in 2020, the marketing channel with the highest engagement and best return is still email marketing.

Yet, I seldom see permission marketing taking place on the career side of sites.

Don't worry. There are still a lot of marketing teams that continue to overlook and undervalue email. Attend any digital marketing conference, and you'll hear something similar: email still works.

This is a big, big, missed opportunity for recruitment marketing. It can also be relatively inexpensive, and you can use existing email marketing platforms that exist.

In fact, Dave Gerhardt, the CMO at Privy and a thought leader on LinkedIn, posted the following around August 3, 2020:

> **Dave Gerhardt** • Following
> CMO at Privy (#1 Sales App on Shopify) | B2B Brand Builder
> 1d
>
> Tik Tok
> Facebook
> Instagram
> Twitter
> LinkedIn
> YouTube
> Podcast
> Events
> Webinars
> Direct Mail
>
> ... but I'd trade them all for an email list.
>
> #marketing
>
> 864 · 184 Comments

Source: LinkedIn

I agree with him. The caveat is that email marketing has to be done correctly.

The list must be built through permission marketing and opt-in. It can't be done from purchased lists.

Permission marketing is usually built through other channels that drive people to your website. The site's content builds trust and proves valuable, and people opt-in to hear from you.

Granted, you have to contend with overly active spam filters, but if you're able to get past those, you don't have to rely on a social media platform's algorithm to decide who and when your message will be delivered.

Email marketing doesn't exist in a vacuum. It's a delivery mechanism for content and valuable information.

In my opinion, the three most crucial components of a digital marketing team are the following people: a design person, a writer/content person, and someone highly adept with email marketing.

If I were building a marketing team from the ground up, those would be my first hires. Paid search and paid search can be cobbled together and can be improved very quickly. They're built on short-term strategies and tactics.

Content, design, and email are part of the long-term strategy, and I would want to get that built and running as soon as possible.

They Want to Hear From You

According to SmashFly's 2020 Recruitment Marketing Benchmark Report, only 43% of the employers interviewed have a "talent network," and of those, only 8% send content other than jobs.

I shouldn't be surprised by this. But I am.

First of all, when you have a team of recruiters who rely on email and messaging to engage with candidates on a 1:1 basis about the open roles they're recruiting for, why wouldn't email marketing play a more prominent role in the engagement of people who have opted-in to hear from you?

If email doesn't work, why aren't recruiters doing something else when they initially contact a candidate?

I know they're not calling each one.

You've done the hard part. You've been able to convince someone to opt-in to a list that will help them learn more about your organization, team, projects, and open roles.

Then nothing happens. The candidate never hears from you other than the sporadic spray and pray of open jobs.

I'm still trying to figure out what the recruitment CRM "AI and machine learning" does to reach the right candidates with the right message.

What messaging?

Compare this to non-recruitment marketing being done at companies.

Nearly 90% of companies engage in email marketing, compared to only 39% of marketers consider using social media to increase brand awareness as a top priority. [20]

That is nearly the opposite of what I'm finding as I learn more about recruitment marketing and employer branding.

Not only that, but 59% of marketers also say that email marketing delivers the highest ROI of any channel, and 81% of businesses use email as their primary customer acquisition channel.[21]

This isn't to say that email should be your only focus, but it's an integral part of your entire recruitment marketing strategy.

---

[20] https://www.marketingsupply.co/blog/most-profitable-digital-marketing-strategies-2019/

[21] https://www.smartinsights.com/email-marketing/email-communications-strategy/emerging-email-marketing-trends-survive-2019-infographic/

It shouldn't only be used at the beginning (as another job broadcasting platform) and end (1:1 email inviting them to the interview process), but as another touchpoint throughout their information gathering and consideration phases.

It should be used to nurture, build trust, and inform. Not to sell.

14

Content Marketing

Content and Brand Journalism

Good, quality, useful content takes time to create. There's usually research involved or interviews and, in some cases, several people involved.

If you think about your audience, they're typically people who want to learn more about your company, your team, and your projects, but they're in no hurry to leave their current role.

They don't want to hear from you every week. Maybe not even every month, but I think a monthly cadence would be useful as a way to keep them engaged and to stay top of mind.

During the 2020 Virtual MozCon conference, Andy Crestodina, Chief Marketing Officer and Co-Founder of Orbit Media Studios provided some tips on the kinds of content that perform well and are of interest to people.

He listed three types of content, specifically:

- Educational or "How-To"
- Identification or Evaluation of Trends
- Research-Based Reports

In the SEO world, inbound links can be a signal of content quality. The more sites that link to an article, the higher the perceived quality by Google and other search engines.

According to Andy, original research attracts more links than anything.

He also gave an excellent tip for coming up with topics when creating originally researched content: think about the things people say or talk about but are rarely backed up by evidence. Go find the evidence and write about it.

Brand Journalism

Ann Handley, in her book *Everybody Writes,* talks about the concept of brand journalists.

Brand journalism is a term created by Larry Light in 2004 when he was the CMO at McDonald's.

Sixteen years later, Larry still believes in the power of brand journalism, maybe more than ever.

In an article he wrote for Forbes in January 2020, he said:

"Brand Journalism can be the most valuable tool in the marketer's advertising and communications toolbox. Brand Journalism captures the interests of consumers who want customized, connective content. Brand Journalism offers the right messages to the right person in the right situation at the right time with the right content in the right format for the right device. It is anything but boring and repetitive."[22]

But what is brand journalism?

According to Thomas Scott (no relation) and Greg Lacour on the website brandjournalists.com:

"Brand Journalism involves telling journalism-style stories about a company that make readers want to know more, stories that don't read like marketing or advertising copy."[23]

As I've mentioned several times, I believe content is the cornerstone of modern marketing.

This is precisely why I would hire a content writer, a design person, and email marketing and social media professionals focusing on audience development (not distribution) as the core of my recruitment marketing team.

Ideally, I would find two people capable of doing all four of these things: a content writer with email marketing experience and a social media professional with design skills.

---

[22] *Brand Journalism is Alive and Well* – Forbes; https://www.forbes.com/sites/larrylight/2020/01/21/brand-journalism-is-alive-and-well/

[23] *What is Brand Journalism?* - https://brandjournalists.com/featured/what-is-brand-journalism/

Content Creation

Content creation and distribution have become the cornerstones of digital marketing, especially inbound marketing.

I've developed a content strategy at my company that has increased our year-over-year organic search traffic by 108%, 47%, and 29%, respectively, from 2018 through 2020.

I'm not trying to toot my own horn, but instead, demonstrate the tremendous impact content can have on driving organic search traffic.

During the writing of this book, I attended the virtual HRTX conference. One of the presentations I sat through was about content. I was excited to hear how content was being used in recruitment marketing.

What I heard was how it was being created by recruiters.

While recruiters should be writing blog posts and creating videos and other content, what they produce should be supplemental to a more robust content strategy.

Given that content is the cornerstone of digital marketing, doing this right will take considerably more time than a recruiter can provide.

They would be a great resource for writing about the interviewing process at your company, including resume tips and other information that would help people interested in joining your company now.

However, by the time someone is reading your content about searching for a job- which is likely the topic recruiters would write about- it may be too late.

When it comes to content, recruiters (unless they're recruiting other recruiters) need to focus more on distributing content and less on the creation of content.

For example, if I'm a marketing professional who isn't looking for a new role, I wouldn't care about job search tips or that your company is hiring. I *would* be interested in knowing about your company's marketing, and the insight people on your marketing team would be willing to share.

The bottom line if I'm interested in your company but not actively seeking another role is that I want to consume content from your company's marketers, not your recruiters.

Over time, if I found the information helpful, it would signal that you have a strong marketing team that's doing fun and exciting work. *That information would put your company on my radar when I'm ready to make a change.*

If you're looking to use content as part of your recruitment marketing, you need to focus on getting the right content in front of the right people and understand what those people are actually interested in based on where they're at in their career. Everyone knows it's crucial to engage way before someone is ready to make a move, and that's why recruitment marketing is so important.

What Will I Be?

Email lists and quality content are the cornerstones of an effective marketing program.

Social media and branding are great, but you aren't in control of who sees your message and when. It's the brand equivalent of spray and pray, which may be why employer branding is more prevalent than recruitment marketing. It translates more closely to the way recruiters have been acting all of these years.

Sure, you can try to put your message in a place where your audience spends time, but it's predicated on hope more than skill.

It's mostly pay-to-play and algorithms that no one fully understands other than the people creating them. It's all assumption.

Too often, it's assumed if you keep showing up in someone's social feed with pictures of your 3 pm Friday keggers and cool Halloween parties, people will jump the next time you post a job.

I see that and want no part of University 2.0.

What I want to see is the work that is being done. How the people at the company – from leadership to potential peers – think about problems and the industry.

Most of all, I want to know what I'll *be* when I get there.

Chances are you'll hire me to *do* almost exactly what I'm doing now. That's how hiring works (and is part of why it's broken).

Will I *be* successful?

Will I *be* challenged?

Will I *be* heard?

Will I *be* valuable?

Will I *be* appropriately compensated for the value I provide?

Will I *be* respected?

Will I *be* included?

Don't get me wrong, people are interested in what they'll do, but they want to know more. It's the intangibles that make working at your company different than another, especially if I can *do* the same thing at both places. But for some reason, the messaging you hear coming from hiring teams and companies are all about the *doing*.

That's why your content and engagement strategy have to be good. You can't continue with the status quo. You need to understand why someone would be interested in your company. Sometimes it's irrational and based on emotion, but marketing is deeply involved in emotion and how people feel.

Someone's reason for wanting to work at a company may differ from why we would work there.

Stop telling *your* story and try to connect with the story they want to write but haven't written yet.

15

Content Distribution and Inbound Marketing

Long Sales Cycles and Risk

There's a lot of chatter in recruitment marketing circles about approaching candidates in the same way you would approach consumers.

I think that's misguided. Job searching is not like going to the grocery store. Yes, you need both food and a job to get by in the world, but they aren't even close when it comes to the implications of bad decisions made in each situation.

If you buy the wrong thing at the grocery store, it may cost you $2. Suppose you make a wrong decision about your next job. In that case, it could cost you thousands of dollars, make your life miserable, and, possibly, destroy friendships and your marriage: much more risk and significantly larger implications.

As I've mentioned throughout my book, I acknowledge that you need a short-term strategy to find and engage candidates like most companies rely on today. That will never change, just as salespeople need to find and engage new leads in a short-term time frame. It's just part of business.

But a big difference between sales and recruiting is the long-term, nurturing process that I've experienced. Or should I say, the lack of a long-term nurturing process when it comes to recruiting?

This is crazy to me. A SaaS salesperson will nurture a lead for months, even years, trying to get someone at a company that brings in $100 million in revenue per year to spend $10,000 on their platform. But a recruiter won't even send a single follow up email a few months after initial contact with a person not in the market for a new role. Not to mention a new role that could impact their lives for years.

Changing jobs and companies carries big implications- especially if relocation is involved.

The higher the stakes and potential risk, the longer the sales cycle. It's not rocket science.

Yet, many recruiters fail to create processes and workflows to enable the kind of follow up needed.

It's not all on the recruiters, though. The majority of the blame falls on recruitment and talent acquisition leaders who focus too much on the short-term numbers and outcomes and don't provide an environment that values long-term relationship building and candidate nurturing.

It's also on the companies whose short-sighted vision can only see what's ahead of them three months at a time and cater more to shareholders than they do to their own employees and, sometimes even their customers.

If these organizations want to do all of the things they say they want to do, including increasing the quality of hires, decreasing the time to fill (or more fashionably called "empty chair time" now), and cutting the amount of money they spend on job postings and tools such as LinkedIn.

If you want to create a recruitment marketing team, it's time to start thinking like marketers.

Multi-Channel Attribution

If you start to think like a marketer, you'll realize that the way people interact and their behavior is often not linear when it comes to digital content. As Adam Gordon, Co-Founder of Candidate.ID put it, "it's like the flight of a bumblebee."

You can try to influence the order with which your audience consumes certain kinds of content (more on that later). But, for the most part, people are all over the place with the way they consume your content, view your site, engage with your social media, and other touchpoints.

Here's an example of the multi-channel attribution that resulted in a website lead conversion at the company I work at, ISM:

| Paid Search | Direct | Organic Search | Paid Search × 2 | Direct | Paid Search | Direct |

Our reporting in Google Analytics measures last-click attribution as the source contributing to our lead, so in this instance, it would show up in our reporting that Paid Search was the channel that delivered this lead. You may notice Direct being the last touchpoint listed above. Direct isn't usually counted in last-touch attribution if a different source immediately precedes it. If Direct is the only source listed, then the conversion will be attributed to it.

This is because direct traffic, as Google measures it, is too much of a wild card. It can mean that the person went directly to your site from a bookmark or by typing in your site's URL, but it can also be a catchall for sources that Google can't directly identify and doesn't know where it came from.

Attribution measurement and weighting is something that marketers currently don't have a standardized way of measuring, so many use last-click attribution. The reason being: it's so damn complicated, and it's hard to understand which source was the one that had the most impact on the person's decision to take an action that turned them into a lead (or applicant in the case of recruitment).

The Marketing Funnel

Even though people flit around the digital world like an unpredictable bee, there is a level of predictability to it that you can take advantage of as a marketer.

Whether you view this as a funnel or some other kind of visual, its core is the same: awareness, consideration, conversion, loyalty, and advocacy.

Another way to think about this and how I most commonly think about it when designing and developing content is TOFU, MOFU, and LOFU/BOFU, which stands for Top-of-Funnel, Middle-of-Funnel, and Lower-Funnel or Bottom-of-Funnel.

> **A Note on Funnels:** As you get more involved in marketing, you'll hear people talk about their disdain for the funnel concept or that they believe there's a different way to look at it. I haven't been convinced yet.
>
> Funnels and a buyer's (or Candidate's) journey aren't precisely the same. More on that later.

Funnels and a buyer's (or Candidate's) journey aren't precisely the same. More on that later.

Where people are in this funnel, at any given time, will predict the type of content they are most interested in and the type of messaging you'll need to incorporate to help 'push' them into the next phase.

Funnels are convenient ways to build a content strategy but shouldn't be confused with the actual steps of a buyer (or candidate) journey.

The Candidate Journey

The company, Candidate.ID, thinks about the funnel, or candidate journey as flowing from Cold to Warm to Hire-Ready.

CONTENT DISTRIBUTION AND INBOUND MARKETING

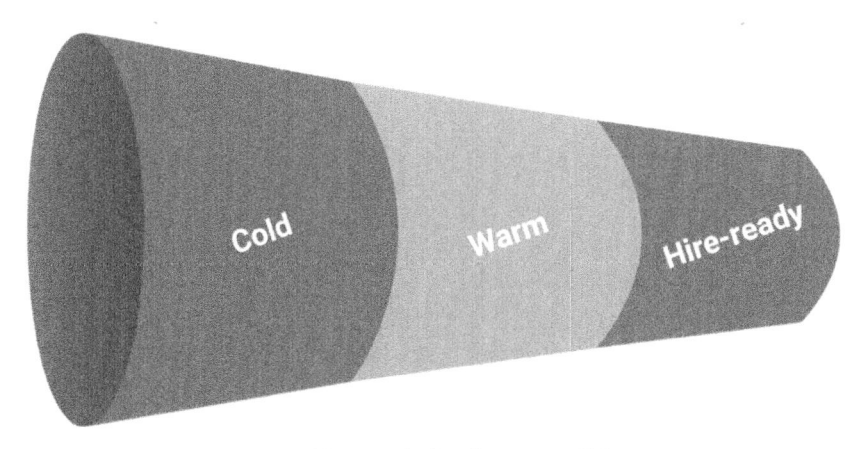

Source: with permission from Candidate.ID

Through testing and the data they've collected in working with numerous clients' content strategy Candidate.ID has developed a content map with the recommended channels, formats, and types of content that is typically most engaged with and useful at each stage:

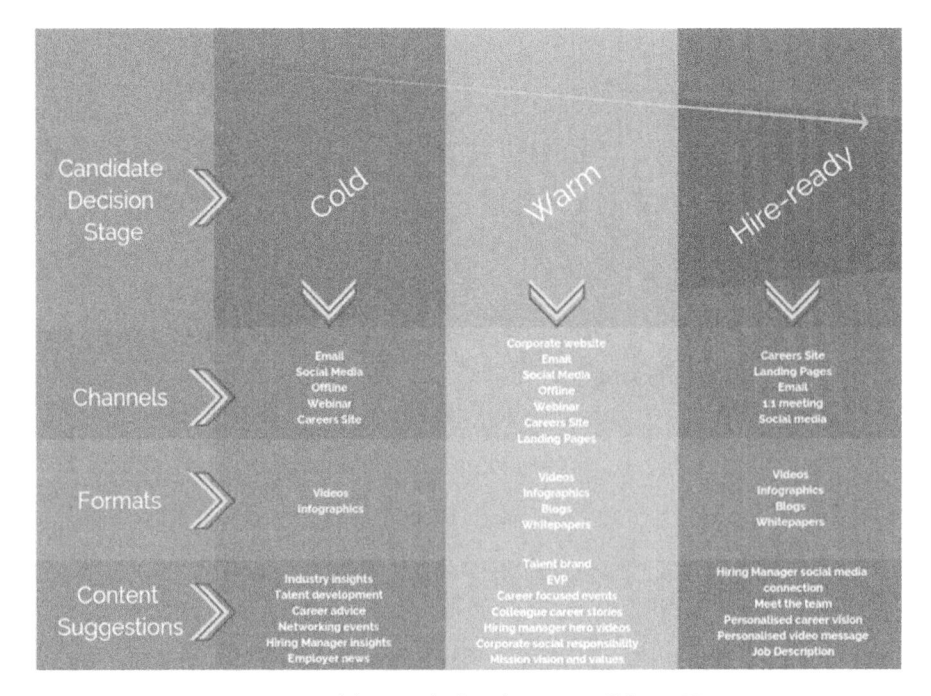

Candidate Decision Stage	Cold	Warm	Hire-ready
Channels	Email Social Media Offline Webinar Careers Site	Corporate website Email Social Media Offline Webinar Careers Site Landing Pages	Careers Site Landing Pages Email 1:1 meeting Social media
Formats	Videos Infographics	Videos Infographics Blogs Whitepapers	Videos Infographics Blogs Whitepapers
Content Suggestions	Industry insights Talent development Career advice Networking events Hiring Manager insights Employer news	Talent brand EVP Career focused events Colleague career stories Hiring manager hero videos Corporate social responsibility Mission vision and values	Hiring Manager social media connection Meet the team Personalised career vision Personalised video message Job Description

Source: with permission from Candidate .ID

The type of messaging and the level of depth your content must go into depends on the company you work for. If you work for a well-known, established company like Microsoft or Amazon, you don't need your awareness content to focus on the brand. You need to focus on increasing awareness around the type of roles available, the work you're doing, lesser-known things like company-led philanthropy and community support, and other similar things.

If you work for a small, lesser-known startup, you'll need to focus more of your awareness content on who you are and what you do.

Similar to the concept of "crossing the chasm" presented in Geoffrey A. Moore's book of the same name, you will need to focus on finding the "early adopters" and engaging with them.

Joining a startup involves risk, just as spending your hard-earned money

CONTENT DISTRIBUTION AND INBOUND MARKETING

on a relatively new, untested new product or service. Not everyone will be interested in taking that kind of risk.

It's important to be aware of this and develop your content strategy and funnel accordingly.

Another way of looking at the customer or candidate journey is through something of an infinite loop. This has been used more commonly in marketing, and I've heard Allyn Bailey, Talent Acquisition Transformation Manager at Intel, talk a lot about this concept.

Here's what it looks like for a candidate:

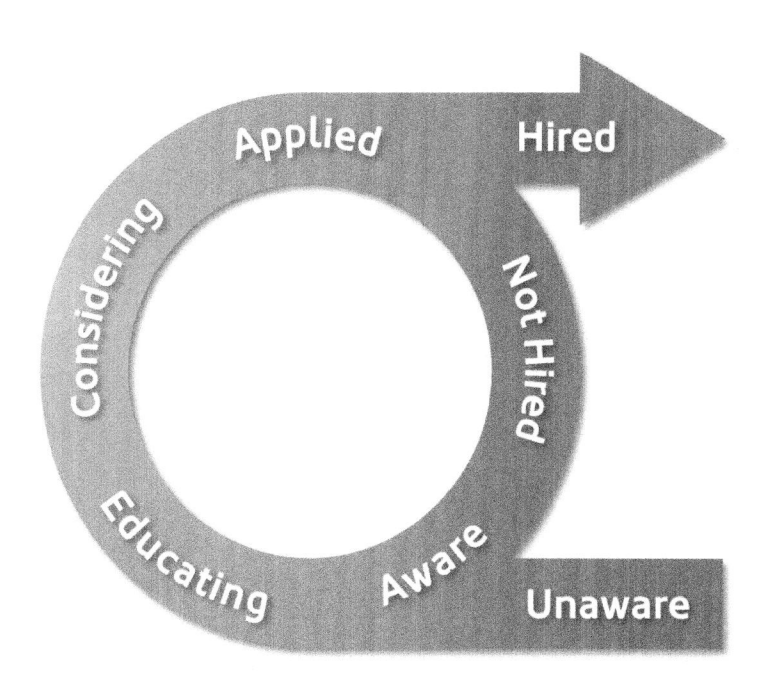

Source: with permission from Candidate .ID

Even when someone's hired, they can re-enter this loop as an employee considering other internal roles. This is similar to how a company would market a new product or service. Maybe, as a consumer, you purchased or didn't purchase an existing product or service, and a new product is launched. In that case, you'll be right back in the loop.

Marketing Automation

As I've immersed myself in the world of recruitment marketing and employer branding, I've noticed that the word 'automation' is becoming a trigger point.

I can only think this is happening because people are either misusing automation- maybe even overusing it – or some people don't fully understand its use and benefits.

If overused, it can seem impersonal from a communication standpoint and can also come across as a little creepy.

However, if used strategically and appropriately, it can become a powerful tool allowing recruiters and recruitment marketers to better engage with candidates, provide a better candidate experience, and save time on routine and repetitive tasks.

What is Marketing Automation

In its most simple form, marketing automation has been around for a very long time. Whenever you've completed a form on a website and immediately received a follow-up email with more information or the next steps someone needs. That's marketing automation.

You've automated a routine marketing task of following up with a lead. You've also created a better customer experience by getting the person what they need or requested as fast as possible.

To a certain degree, this kind of follow up and automation is expected by people. If you fill out a form or subscribe to a newsletter (or apply to a job), not getting an immediate, automated follow-up may seed some doubt in your mind about the person or company you've just interacted with online.

You've probably heard of email 'drip' campaigns, which are a series of email follow-ups spread out over time, each one either building on the previous one or nurturing a lead closer to a lower-funnel (LOFU) activity.

Again, not new, and nearly everyone knows it's an automated campaign.

Over the past decade, marketing automation has moved beyond email platforms like Constant Contact and MailChimp and has become too sophisticated and more complex.

As a marketer who has researched and implemented two different marketing automation platforms at my current company, ISM, I can tell you, there's no shortage of options.

The challenge is that CRM companies have acquired several of the best platforms since they could not (or were unwilling to) develop their own. You might as well buy versus build and not "reinvent the wheel."

These acquisitions have made these platforms more suitable for only one CRM. For example, the Indianapolis-based marketing firm, ExactTarget, purchased the marketing automation company, Pardot, for $95 million in October 2012. Just eight months later, in June 2013, CRM behemoth, Salesforce, swooped in to acquire ExactTarget, primarily for access to Pardot, for $2.5 billion.[24]

Not a bad return on investment for ExactTarget executives.

That was on the tail of Oracle purchasing the marketing automation platform, Eloqua, for nearly $871 million in December of 2012.[25]

These acquisitions were taking marketing automation in the backward direction that has plagued recruitment technology for years. One of the most stifling aspects of recruitment technology has been the lack of open infrastructures. Basically, the inability of many applicant tracking systems (ATS), essentially the ERPs of recruiting, to play well and connect with other platforms.

Now, if you really wanted to use Pardot, you probably should change your CRM to Salesforce.

Why were these large companies willing to pay so much for these marketing automation platforms?

Because of how powerful they were in creating efficiencies and more significant opportunities around lead nurturing.

One of the most potent aspects of most marketing automation platforms is creating lead scoring based on the recent website activity of a known lead.

---

[24] https://www.bizjournals.com/atlanta/blog/atlantech/2012/10/atlantas-pardot-acquired-by.html

[25] https://www.oracle.com/corporate/pressrelease/oracle-buys-eloqua-122012.html

How It Works

With marketing automation, once someone opts-in, usually by way of completing a form on your website, you can now see how they interact with your website and content.

For example, the pages they visit, the videos they watch, the case studies they download, and other similar activities.

You can provide scores for each type of activity. Some behaviors indicate an increased interest and may hint that the person is entering or are in the 'Consideration Phase' of the buyer's or candidate's journey.

For example, you could weight each pageview as 1 point and 10 points if someone watches a video. If they visit a job description, 15 points. This adds up over time to create a score.

My lead nurturing team pays close attention to our lead scoring. When someone reaches a 150 or higher score, we notify the salesperson tied to that account and recommend they contact them through email or phone to check in and see if they can offer any assistance.

We could also create an automated email that could be sent out shortly after the person reaches the threshold score of 150. In my opinion, the key is to create a delay between the time they attain the score and when they are contacted.

By informing the salesperson of their activity, the resulting email and the timing seem more natural and individualized.

However, if you're dealing with a high volume of emails that would result from this kind of behavior, then make the adjustment and create the automated follow up. That's what it's designed to do.

The same can be done when it comes to recruiting. That would be an excellent time to try to schedule a phone call.

There's a host of reasons they could be more engaged on your site or career site and not apply. It could mean they're interested in a role at your company, but they aren't finding the right type of position to pursue.

Depending on the content they engaged with on your site, you could also create an automated email that provides links to other, similar content or content that may not be available on your website but is very valuable.

The sky is the limit with what you can do and how you can use marketing automation for good.

If used correctly, marketing automation can save a tremendous amount of time, further engage the candidates, and create a more personalized and better candidate experience.

Segmentation and Strategic Content Delivery

Segmentation and content delivery are the keys to any successful email marketing campaign, and when using marketing automation.

What is segmentation? Segmentation is the process of grouping people based on similar characteristics. These characteristics could be job title, location, company (when executing an ABM campaign), or their position within the buyer's journey, which is based on behavior.

By creating and maintaining segmented lists, you can deliver content and messaging that those people will be most interested in consuming.

Segmentation is done both manually and automatically when using marketing automation or an email marketing platform.

These lists are fluid, never static, because people are continuously moving between different levels of the buyer's journey. The idea, from a marketer's standpoint, is to be the guide in the journey.

By understanding the buying process, or in the case of recruitment marketing, the job-seeking process, you can deliver content that will be of most interest to that person at that moment but also ties into the next steps.

This is considered lead or candidate nurturing.

It can be a long process, depending on where people are in their interest level and desire to make a change.

But remember when we were talking about what marketing is? Marketing is about making change. Marketers make change happen.

Change in this instance is gradual but planned.

Change is moving the lead or candidate through the different phases – from awareness to engagement to consideration to purchase or hire.

At each phase, you're creating an environment of change.

To successfully execute a lead or candidate nurturing program, you must understand your customers and how they became customers.

You need to know what problems you're solving for them, what objections and doubts they will have along the way, and why and how they make decisions. Do others influence this process?

How can you influence this process?

What information do they need and want as they move from one stage to the next?

What questions will they have?

What parts of your website do they visit when they're at each stage?

How much time does it typically take for someone to go from the awareness stage to purchase or hire? What about if you meet them at another stage?

This can all be executed through a well thought out marketing automation platform.

Do you know the decision-making process your customers or candidates went through before becoming a customer or hire?

If not, it may be time to start talking with them. You can also talk to people as they're moving through the process. What questions do they ask the recruiters they speak with?

You can create content that answers these questions ahead of time. What if your recruiter was able to send over a PDF or point the candidate to a page on your site that talked about these FAQs ahead of their interview? What if this could be sent automatically based on an interview scheduled through or documented in your CRM?

It can.

Do you think this use of automation creates a better candidate experience? I do.

Retargeting

Retargeting is an advertising strategy used to stay top of mind and encourage someone to come back to your website and take some desired action, such as make a purchase or complete a lead gen form.

This is usually done in the form of display ads or paid social ads. When you visit the website of a company engaged in retargeting, a cookie is placed on your machine – phone, tablet, or desktop. This cookie is tied to an advertising network, and whenever you go to another site that has advertising through this network, you'll see ads for the company or brand you were visiting.

According to digitalmarketingjobs.com, retargeted ads on Facebook are 76% more likely to get clicks than regular ad campaigns. When it comes to lead gen or purchases, 70% of people who see retargeted ads are 70% more likely to convert.

You may be asking, "why is retargeting in a chapter about inbound and content distribution if it's a form of advertising?"

Remarketing is done because the people it's intended to reach visited your site and didn't become a lead or a candidate.

The goal of retargeting is to stay top-of-mind and encourage the visitor to come back and further engage, ultimately becoming a lead (or applicant).

Retargeting bridges the gap between engagement and conversion and is an effective form of nurturing.

Benefits of Retargeting

People often arrive on your site through a disruption such as a Facebook or LinkedIn ad or display ad. They weren't actively seeking out your products or services at the time, but your ad caught their attention. They may not be in a position to make a purchase or take any other action.

That doesn't mean that they will never be in a position to take action. Sometimes the timing needs to be better.

By staying top of mind through display ads shown on other websites, you will better ensure that your messaging and brand are in front of them when they are ready to take action.

Retargeting and Recruiting

Retargeting can be equally beneficial, if not more so when it comes to recruiting. Often, someone will come across an open role that interests them, but they may not be in a position to apply at that moment.

That could be because of numerous factors, such as they're on a mobile device, and the application process isn't mobile-friendly. They could be required to upload their resume, but they are either at work and don't have a copy they can upload or are on a mobile device.

Maybe they need to give it more thought before committing to applying and going through the interview process.

It could be that they don't have the time to apply.

Regardless of their situation, it's essential to stay in front of them and be in the right place at the right time when they can apply.

In this situation, retargeting can increase the chances you don't miss out on a great candidate because of bad timing.

16

Measurement and Analytics

An Introduction to Measurement

Modern digital marketing is complex. Consumers (including candidates) are more savvy and skeptical.

Not to mention, the importance of making such an impactful decision as to where you'll work leads to long sales (or recruiting) cycles.

Yet, the majority of recruitment is done quickly and transactionally.

There's a myth that effective sourcing can uncover "passive" candidates that aren't engaged with other companies and get them into their current interview process with little competition from other companies who may also be interested in hiring that person.

That's nothing more than wishful thinking.

The minute that person decides to talk with you about your role, they will likely go out and see what else is out there and start applying to other roles.

The only real competitive advantage is to build an enduring professional relationship with the best talent -whether they're looking to make a move in 6 months or 2 years- and ensuring the interview process and candidate experience are well designed and consistent at every touchpoint.

You could spend years developing a solid relationship with a candidate only to have a bad interview experience completely ruin it.

Building a great marketing program -whether it's related to recruitment, a product, or a service – takes time, and not all markets are created equal.

Sales and Marketing Aren't Measured the Same So Why is Recruitment Different?

One of the biggest hurdles to a successful talent marketing program is the uncertainty around what to measure and what matters.

If you were to imagine marketing teams at companies being built through the transitioning of salespeople, you would probably be right to think that they would likely fail. Or at least sputter early on.

Salespeople, especially closers, are wired differently than marketing professionals.

Salespeople have one or two touchpoints – email and phone. The same is true with recruiters (I'm lumping messaging on social in with email here).

Their metrics are different from marketers: demos, quotes, and closed deals.

For recruiters, it's phone interviews, interviews, offers, and hires.

By the time customers and candidates engage and talk with salespeople and recruiters, there are usually strong buying signals and interest.

When it comes to marketing, there's the possibility that zero interest exists. Hell, it's likely the person doesn't even know who their company, product, or service is.

If you think about it in dating terms, that's like asking a random person you pass on a sidewalk out on a date. It probably isn't going to have a positive outcome.

It's also possible that the person may know who you are and what you're selling, but they do not need or want it now.

As a marketer, you hope that there is at least interest in revisiting it down the road. They're just not ready to buy (or leave their current role) at this time.

Marketers have a gazillion touchpoints that happen at varying degrees of awareness and interest.

Measurement – More Than Leads (Candidates)

Let's take email marketing through the use of permission-based lists.

Ultimately, we want people to move from these lists into the lead or applicant stage. But in the meantime, we'll use email marketing to nurture them, build trust, help them decide if we're for them, and be in the right place with the right message at the right time.

That last part is much easier through email marketing than random follow-ups.

This can take time, and that's the benefit of email: it allows you to directly engage with candidates without the need to worry about algorithms not delivering your message to the people who want to hear it.

The keys to email marketing are to provide value to the reader and be consistent.

Finding a cadence that works for you and sticking to it will show much better results (and result in fewer unsubscribes) than randomly sending out an email each week for a few weeks, then nothing for another two months.

So, if leads are the ultimate objective, but those take time to acquire, what else should we pay attention to?

There are several metrics to pay attention to, and the importance of each will change based on the email copy and expected action taken.

Fundamental Email Marketing Metrics:

1. Conversion Rate: This measures the percentage of email recipients who clicked on a link you've shared and completed a desired action on your site, such as applied to a role or signed up for a webinar or event.

2. List Growth: This metric has nothing to do with the emails being sent out or their copy and messaging. But this is the second most important metric to track behind lead/applicant conversion rate. This is how you eventually scale your email marketing, and, as the list grows, a pattern of consistent conversions will begin to appear. You can track total growth over time, month-over-month growth, as well as the acceleration rate. Keep in mind, you'll want to track the net growth, which takes into account the number of unsubscribes you have.

3. Clickthrough Rate (CTR): You're probably wondering why open rate isn't next. Open rate is one of the most overrated and unreliable metrics. More on that later. CTR is important if you're objective is to drive people to a landing page, content on your website, or even a site you don't own. Clickthrough rate is the percentage of email recipients who clicked on one or more of the external links you've provided in the email.

4. **Bounce Rate:** Keeping a clean list is essential. You don't want to send emails to accounts that are bouncing. This is calculated by:

(Number of bounced emails ÷ Number of emails sent) x 100

5. **Sharing/Forwarding Rate:** A great way to grow your email list is with your current subscribers' help. If they find something useful and share it with others, that's a great indicator of the kind of content that resonates and will help grow your list. It's also particularly crucial if your email's goal is to encourage shares and forwards (obviously).

6. **ROI:** This is something that is usually tied to revenue with companies marketing products or services, but in recruitment, this could be measured in several ways, including how many subscribers moved into the interview phase or how many were hired. This tracking could be more manual, depending on the ATS you're using and how openly it connects to other platforms. Most, sadly, are very bad at this.

7. **Unsubscribe Rate:** This is an important metric to measure for several reasons. The most important is to measure the value of the content you're sharing and the frequency you're sharing it. Competition is at an all-time high for people's attention, and providing value in every email you send is important. If the subscribers fail to find your email content valuable, they'll unsubscribe. If you're sending messages out too frequently, this may cause some people to unsubscribe. An important thing to note is that unsubscribing should not be something you try to maintain at zero. It's actually good if people unsubscribe because they've determined that you're not for them. That's a good thing because we want the quality of our list to be maintained. People who aren't interested and no longer engage will bring down all of our

metrics.

8. Open Rate: Here it is. Finally. The most overrated metric in email marketing. Open rate is something to keep an eye on, but don't make big decisions based on it. Also, ignore benchmarks for what your open rate should be. They're worthless. Every industry and market is different. Ignore them. Seriously. DO NOT make this your top KPI. Open rate measures just what it sounds like; the number of email recipients who opened your email. Given how some email clients automatically open an email after the previous message has been opened or moved, this will inflate the number of opens. Just because it was opened doesn't mean it was read or even looked at. Now, if you do see a meager open rate of, let's say, 10% or less, then you may want to dive deeper into the subject lines you're using and how you're representing yourself through the sender name that shows up in their inbox.

What to Measure – Using Marketing Analytics

Ultimately, we'd like hires to be the primary KPI of every marketing channel we use. However, it all depends on how well your applicant tracking system (ATS) tracks analytics, especially traffic sources.

Applicant Tracking Systems, for the longest time, have been the most significant innovation killer in recruitment. Most are closed systems that don't play well with 3rd party tools and platforms. This is the complete opposite of most of the commonly used CRMs available to sales organizations.

However, this is changing, and things are finally moving in the right direction. Several applicant tracking systems are now designed to be open platforms, including Greenhouse and Workday.

If you're in the market for a new ATS, you should consider this one of the most critical features.

Using Marketing Analytics

There are several website analytics tools on the market, but Google Analytics is still the go-to solution for most companies.

It's free, powerful, and robust. (Although there's a paid version called Google Analytics 360, I feel Google will start pushing onto people, especially if ad revenue ever starts to fall.)

— — — —

A Note About Recent Changes to Google Analytics:

Some big changes are coming to Google Analytics through the introduction of Google Analytics 4 (or GA4). GA4 will become less of a reporting platform and has tighter integration with Google's Data Studio for report creation.

As of this book's writing, GA4 hasn't been received well by the digital marketing community. This will be something to continue to keep an eye on as it could change the digital marketing analytics landscape considerably.

— — — —

I would highly recommend designing and developing your website's careers portion just as you would any other page or section of your site and adding Google Analytics to it.

Depending on your ATS, your tracking may break once someone applies to an open role, but there are workarounds for this, although not ideal.

Many commercial and non-profit websites have a similar issue when using a third-party payment processing or e-commerce platform that forces people off of their website and onto the third-party platform.

A number of these platforms, like some ATS', allow you to connect your Google Analytics by using your UA number, the equivalent of your Google Analytics account number. This works with GA to enable the pass-through of your data into the third-party platform without losing the crucial last step, which is usually one of, if not your primary, KPIs.

This is crucial to understanding where your career site traffic is coming from to give you a way to measure your marketing activities' effectiveness. All of your content should be on your career site, and you should be able to see which sources not only sent the most traffic but which ones sent the most engaged traffic.

By engaged, I mean, how long did they stay on your site or page? Was it long enough to read your blog or watch your video? Did they visit more than one page? Did they click the 'apply' button? Subscribe to your email list? Did they come from an email you sent?

Similar to some brand marketing, where you cannot measure its impact on revenue directly, you can use your past data as a baseline to see if any 'lift' can be measured.

Lift is just an increase in sales or revenue, or in the case of recruitment, applicants that can't directly be attributed to something routine or 'normal.' It's a speculative metric and nothing to weigh too heavily. Still, it can sometimes be used to get a sense of whether your brand or marketing activities impact your bottom line when you can't directly measure it.

IV

Part Four

17

Becoming a Marketer and Building a Team

A Marketer's Mindset

During the writing of this book, I attended a two-day virtual marketing conference called MozCon. It's one of the more well-known digital marketing conferences that occur each year. Even though it's hosted in Seattle and has been local for me, I've never been because the content seemed to skew toward SEO (search engine optimization) -my focus has been paid search, paid social, and other digital advertising.

This year, it was virtual and about 10x cheaper than usual, so I decided to attend. Plus, I enjoy marketing conferences. Focusing entirely on marketing for a couple of days and learning from other people usually invigorates me and sparks a lot of great ideas.

I can't speak for the content of past years, but the topics weren't as SEO-heavy as I thought they were going to be. There have been talks on paid search, content, and brand.

As I've watched the presentations, I've been asking myself, "how could I use this in my current marketing role, and how could this also be used in recruiting and retention?"

Thinking about this made me curious about how many recruitment marketing or employer branding folks attended. So, I went to the attendee page and searched. Zero recruitment marketing people. Disappointing, but not unexpected.

When I searched 'employer branding,' I was surprised to not only find people but to find eight people from the same company – T-Mobile, a Seattle-based company.

Of course, they were the only employer branding folks attending and, the fact they had that many employer branding people piqued my interest. I reached out to one of them, a Sr Employer Brand Manager, to introduce myself and see if we could chat sometime after the conference. I also took down the names and titles of the others to contact them after the conference.

None of them replied to me.

It's taken me 275 words to get to my resulting thought: do people in recruitment marketing view themselves as marketers or just another part of recruiting?

Toward the end of my recruiting days, when I became more confident in my marketing skills and more knowledgeable, I started to view myself as a marketer who happened to be in a recruiting role. This way of thinking was a pretty dramatic shift because it changed the way I looked at things. It affected my decision-making, strategies, and tactics.

For example, in 2010, while I was a contract recruiter for Cricket Wireless, they were under pressure to hire a lot of people in their retail locations for the holidays. Even though my focus was on VP- and Director-level folks and technical people, I had an idea to use Facebook's advertising features. These features were new at the time but were more targeted than any other form of digital advertising because they had so much information about the people in their network.

So, I created Facebook ads targeting people within a particular demographic, within specific geographic areas, who had retail experience.

I left to join Microsoft before I could see the results, but I'm pretty sure not many people were using Facebook ads in 2010 for recruiting purposes. Probably because there weren't many marketers in recruiting that knew how it worked.

This mindset would continue with me through my time at Microsoft and later when I was doing some recruitment projects for Booking. com.

In 2011, shortly after joining Microsoft, I helped build a blog that my team could use to attract talent to our group and encouraged some of the other recruiters to contribute to it. I also created a private group on LinkedIn that was built more like a community. People could join and be able to ask questions and have open conversations without their bosses listening in. I monitored it to ensure people in management or leadership roles at the companies people in the group worked at couldn't join to keep the conversations open. Since most of our open positions were never for people at that level, this was pretty easy to do.

I also was a frequent contributor to the Microsoft Jobs Blog, and some of the content I wrote was the most viewed and engaged content across the blog. At least that's what I've been told.

I also started the Windows Jobs social media channels on Twitter, LinkedIn, and Facebook and used a marketing tool from Moz called FollowerWonk to find people to engage with through their bio search and to gain other insight through the analytics of our connections as well as competitor's connections.

I'm not saying this to toot my own horn, rather provide an example of how I was thinking back then because I had become more knowledgeable around digital marketing through consulting I was doing on the side. I was eager to learn and spent my evenings and weekends in the weeds of digital marketing, getting my hands dirty, and learning.

Lack of Diverse Experience and Technology

An observation I had while in recruiting was how myopic the diversity of experience was throughout recruitment and HR.

It seemed to be pretty rare that those in management and leadership roles had done anything besides recruitment or HR at any other point in their careers.

When I spoke with Lori Sylvia, the Founder of Rally Recruitment Marketing, she described herself as an 'outsider,' meaning she was a marketer who became involved with the technology side of recruitment marketing.

One of her biggest surprises was how slow recruiting organizations seemed to embrace new technology and change. I witnessed this during my time as a recruiter as well.

Technology is a big reason for the lack of progress in recruitment marketing, at least that's my hypothesis and what I hope to expose. Lori agreed.

Applicant tracking systems, essentially the equivalent of an ERP system for data, were expected to be used as a CRM, despite lacking many of the key features needed to do even the most basic CRM functionality. On top of that, many are archaic, bloated, and mostly, if not entirely, closed systems.

Meaning they don't play well with other software.

This is quite the opposite of modern CRM used by most marketing and sales organizations. The MarTech (marketing technology) universe now includes over 8,000 tools and platforms as of 2020, and many of them could be very useful in recruitment marketing. With a closed system, these would become more difficult to use.[26]

In an article written on Forbes.com, James McDermott, CEO and Co-Founder of Lytics, said:

"Marketers need a CRM platform that supports the data sources they have today. They need a solution that can take an intelligent profile of their customers and execute personalized, orchestrated campaigns seamlessly across various tools, from email to mobile push to real-time content recommendations. They probably won't find that functionality in an integrated suite."[27]

This is being said of marketing organizations. Organizations that are usually light years ahead of recruiting organizations. It's not hard to see how the gap between recruitment marketing and boots-on-the-ground digital marketing will continue to grow.

Even some CRMs are unable to keep up with the influx of new MarTech platforms and tools, and it's leaving some marketing organizations in the dust.

According to Scott Brinker of chiefmartec.com, the MarTech stack grew nearly

---

[26] Source: https://chiefmartec.com/2020/04/marketing-technology-landscape-2020-martech-5000/

[27] Source: https://www.forbes.com/sites/forbestechcouncil/2020/03/26/the-traditional-martech-stack-has-just-been-toppled/#8133954462cd

14% between 2019 and 2020.[28] In 2011, there were about 150 MarTech tools and platforms. Now there are more than 8,000.

That's mind-blowing growth, and the options ranging from advertising and promotion to data to content and experience to social media management to email marketing is head-spinning.

What If...?

Now that you're thinking like a marketer, it's time to start acting like one.

What if you could develop a part of your recruitment program that lowered your time to hire?

What if you implemented a program that could drastically lower your cost per hire?

What if that same program could increase the quality of your hires?

But wait, there's more.

What if this same program improved the candidate experience and lead people who don't work at your company to talk about how remarkable it is? I'm talking about people who interviewed but didn't get the job.

What if candidates already had a great understanding of what the work culture and environment are like?

---

[28] Source: https://chiefmartec.com/2020/04/marketing-technology-landscape-2020-martech-5000/

What if they had a sampling of the type of work they would be engaged with?

What if they had become so familiar with people on the team that they felt like they already knew them- how they think, how they work?

What if this program could cut down on the amount of ramp-up and onboarding time needed to get a person on track in their new role?

That's what recruitment marketing has the potential to do. If done right.

Like nearly everything else worthwhile in life, it takes time to build and get rolling.

Once rolling, though, it can become a consistent source of quality hires.

We're talking at least a year, not a quarter. The longer you stick with it, not only will it become immensely more valuable, but it will also become a very tangible competitive advantage.

This is the vision I've had for talent acquisition for years. The lack of companies' commitment to long-term strategies eventually pushed me out altogether and into marketing full time.

However, I haven't given up on this becoming a reality, which is why I wrote this book.

You Wouldn't Hire a Butcher to Be Your Five-Star Chef

So, why would you hire a salesperson to build your marketing program?

No one that I know in the marketing world would do that, but it happens at companies all of the time when they decide to build a recruitment marketing and employer branding program.

Sales and marketing are different. The people who work in sales are different than those who are in marketing.

I know this because I've been in both. I can do sales, but I'm not a salesperson.

Yes, at the end of the day, they both have the same business objective. Increasing the profitable revenue of a company.

Without this, companies can't exist.

But our mentalities couldn't be more different.

"Always be closing" is the mantra of sales.

"Always be testing" is the mantra of marketing.

If they were farmers, marketing would be planting the seeds and caring for the crop all summer long. Sales would be the combine, harvesting the crop in the early Fall. Monetizing it.

I have a decade of marketing experience, not including the hefty bill I paid for an MBA that focused on the discipline.

All of that, and I'm still learning what marketing really is.

I also have nearly 15 years of recruitment experience. Even when I've not been a formal recruiter by profession, I've still been involved. Occasionally, donning my recruitment hat at the small company I work at.

Before all of this, I was in sales.

I'm writing all of this to say: marketing and sales are fundamentally different.

I'm also saying that recruiting and marketing are also fundamentally different.

So why do so many companies- especially Fortune 500 companies – try to turn recruiters into marketers? So, often, that's the least experienced person on the team you could tap for a role like this.

It's usually the young, fresh-out-of-college person. Surely, they're really good at social media. They're hired!

Marketing is not social media. Social media is a channel for distribution and some engagement.

It's one small piece of marketing.

But yet, that's what I keep seeing at the heart of so many recruitment marketing and employer branding programs.

I recently asked someone who used to be part of a large, internationally recognized company's employment branding team how they nurtured candidates. He mentioned this was done through social media.

Social media is built on a foundational algorithm.

An algorithm you have zero control over. You're going to rely on an algorithm to nurture candidates?

I'm not singling out this company because I've come to realize through my research that this is the norm. Especially, and most shockingly, for large, Fortune 500 corporations. Companies who have access to a wealth of marketing and branding resources but choose to assemble their recruitment marketing teams as if they were a small, fledgling company struggling to pay the bills.

The reason for this is the mindset.

These companies are asking salespeople (aka recruiters) to build marketing programs.

Or they're hiring marketing professionals with brand marketing experience to build a direct marketing and nurturing program.

The square pegs continue to be hired to fill the round holes.

This is evident when the hottest recruitment tech on the market is a CRM.

In my world, the marketing world, a CRM is a sales platform. Marketers rarely use a CRM other than for reporting.

Only salespeople would think a CRM is the cornerstone of a marketing program.

My world is made up of a plethora of platforms and tools. Marketing is a conglomerate of things that make up the different touchpoints a prospective customer might encounter on their way to becoming (and staying) a customer.

This includes SEO, paid search (Google Ads and Bing Ads for those not familiar with the term), paid social, content (including blogs, whitepapers, ebooks, infographics, and other useful content), email marketing, marketing automation, and organic social among others.

Of these, organic social is the weakest channel because it's powered by an algorithm that allows you to only reach anywhere from 2% to 10% of the people interested in hearing from you. Those are people who have said they want to hear from you. And they don't because the social platform is holding back your exposure to the other 90%-98% of your audience unless you pay.

Yet, social remains the go-to marketing channel for most employment branding and recruitment marketing teams. Meanwhile, if those same people who have chosen to follow your company on social were part of an email list, you would reach nearly 100% of them with your messaging every time.

Email marketing continues to deliver the best results, but yet is seen as 'old school' or not as sexy as the other channels. This continues to blow me away and is also a challenge among digital marketing teams.

It's not the sexiest of digital channels, but unsexy just works most of the time.

Most of the time, companies have people (or partners) who specialize in each one of these areas.

One last note on email...one of the hottest trends right now is for companies to spin up companies based entirely on email newsletters. Take Morning Brew, for example.

It's beginning to rival the Wall Street Journal as a place people turn to to get financial and market news and updates.

Morning Brew is expected to see revenue of around $20 million in 2020, and Insider Inc. recently purchased a majority share of the company for $75 million.[29]

Email marketing still works- if done right.

---

[29] https://www.axios.com/insider-inc-buys-majority-stake-morning-brew-e6ec0673-4354-4bc7-9feb-e0b149508c9a.html

18

The Future of Recruitment Marketing

Is It Impossible or Just Difficult?

Dorie Clark is a recognized expert on personal branding and reinventing your career. She's written over 200 articles for HBR on the topic alone.

If you're unfamiliar with her books, *Re-Inventing You, Stand Out,* and *Entrepreneurial You,* I would recommend giving them a read.

When it comes to helping your idea or business stand out, she talks a lot about finding a niche and looking for opportunities to provide value in a way that may not currently exist.

When exploring possible niches and opportunities, she asks you to think about what people in your industry should be doing but aren't.

Can you dig deeper into the reason(s) why they're not doing those things?

Most importantly, she says, ask yourself, "are other people not doing it because it's impossible, or is it just difficult?"

As I've mentioned, my primary goal of writing this book was to better understand recruitment marketing and, to some extent, employer branding in its current state.

I wanted to better understand how marketing principles are being implemented and executed, what could be done better, and where an opportunity may exist to take it to the next level of its evolution as a legitimate discipline.

As I've talked with those I interviewed for the book and explored what companies are currently doing, I've been looking for gaps. Gaps where things aren't quite equating with what marketing teams are doing. Potential missed opportunities for organizations.

I discovered the same gaps that existed back when I was a recruiter from 2004 through 2015. The most significant and most glaring missed opportunity comes in the form of permission marketing and candidate nurturing.

There's a lot of emphasis on the top-of-funnel (TOFU) activity and generating awareness or the employer branding piece. This puts an unusually high priority on social media, which seems to be the primary focus of most large brands who, ironically, really don't need to build awareness about their brand.

Most companies I've found may have someone running their employer branding, but there's no focus on other recruitment marketing activities. This is a tremendous missed opportunity.

The other place with a high degree of focus and emphasis, not surprisingly, is the bottom of funnel (BOFU) activity – generating applicants.

The Biggest Opportunity that Exists in Recruitment Marketing Today

Do you see what's missing? The top-of-funnel and bottom-of-funnel are firmly represented. What about the middle-of-funnel activity? Virtually non-existent.

This part is nearly universally skipped in hopes that awareness activity will generate leads. That rarely happens in marketing, especially B2B marketing. Why should this be any different when it comes to hiring people?

An extraordinary amount of time and money is invested in these TOFU and BOFU activities and is wasted when a MOFU strategy doesn't exist. These candidates sit, collecting dust, in an ATS or worse, a CRM which doubles as ATS/Black Hole 2.0.

Earlier in the book, I discussed the value of an owned audience compared to a rented audience. There's some real gold in your applicant tracking systems and CRMs being wasted, and I have to ask why?

Is it because it's impossible, or is it just too difficult to build a program around this?

An owned audience is one of the most significant competitive advantages a marketing organization has. Outside of driving revenue, building an owned audience is the second most valuable activity.

If you're struggling to prove the value of your recruitment marketing program, ignoring your most valuable asset may not be helping.

Where will Recruitment Marketing Innovation Happen? Hint: Not Where You Think

Throughout my research into recruitment marketing and employer branding as I've written my book, I've noticed a focus on enterprise companies and what they're doing.

I get it. They're well known and have established brands and followings. They typically have larger budgets than smaller companies and more people to convert into recruitment marketers.

However, the more I think about the discipline of recruitment marketing, how early on we are in defining what it is, and how it fits into the scheme of things, the more I think that meaningful change isn't going to happen at the enterprise level.

I've been thinking about this in the same way that Geoffrey Moore illustrated the technology adoption lifecycle in his book *Crossing the Chasm*.

Although it's an older book, it remains a cornerstone read for most business school students and should be read by all entrepreneurs and professional marketers. It has withstood the test of time.

Here's a graphical representation of what the technology adoption lifecycle looks like:

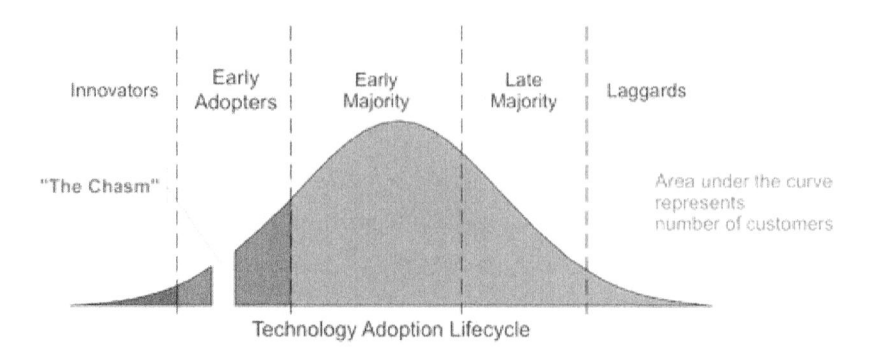

Technology (or solution) adoption process, as described in Geoffrey Moore's book Crossing the Chasm. The chart shows a bell curve split into five sections: Innovators, Early Adopters, Early Majority, Late Majority, and Laggards. The area under the curve represents the number of customers. The Early Adopters section is itself split into two sub-sections between which is "The Chasm"[30]

This principle doesn't only apply to technology. It can apply to the adoption of a new program or discipline.

I would consider most enterprise companies in the "Early Majority" and "Late Majority" phases of incorporating recruitment marketing. They're more risk-averse and need social proof that it works. There's more bureaucracy and more focus on short-term results, in line with their business models of serving shareholders first.

SMBs are more likely to be in the "Innovators" and "Early Adopters" phases. This is where innovation and real change happens.

---

[30] Source: Wikimedia Commons; Private conversation with Craig Chelius; February 10, 2009

https://commons.wikimedia.org/wiki/File:Technology-Adoption-Lifecycle.png

https://creativecommons.org/licenses/by/3.0/deed.en

These companies are nimble, more agile, and more open to testing and experimentation. They tend to focus more on their customers and have more of a long-term outlook.

I realize I'm making an assertion that may be way off, but right now, I believe this is going to be where recruitment marketing is transformed into what it will eventually become.

The discipline of recruitment marketing feels like it's in a bit of a predicament. People are unsure of how it fits into their organization, why they need to spend the money on it, and, most importantly, what they'll tell their boss to secure the budget and time to make it work.

Recruitment marketing and employer branding are long-term strategies requiring time to build the momentum needed to show results.

Time is often a luxury most talent acquisition professionals in enterprise organizations don't have.

This is why, if recruitment marketing is going to turn the corner and 'cross the chasm' into the world of enterprise companies, it's going to have to start with SMBs.

We, as the innovators in the discipline, need to turn our focus to partnering with SMBs. This is where the 'magic' is going to happen.

Recruitment Marketing and Employer Branding for Non-Enterprise Companies

There are definitely pros and cons to both situations. Enterprise-level companies are often big brands. They're established and known, if not household names among people.

This can be negative if their brand has a negative sentiment within the marketplace. Hiring great people is the best way to change a company's reputation, but it can be a Catch-22.

Great people don't want to work at a place with a bad reputation.

You also have politics and bureaucracy to contend with in most enterprise companies. Layers upon layers of people to go through to get anything done. It reminds me of when I used to work for the government.

From 1999 to 2000, I was a NEPA Compliance Specialist for a government contractor tasked with cleaning up the Rocky Flats Plant, just outside of Golden, Colorado. NEPA is an acronym for National Environmental Protection Act, which is a law established to essentially keep the federal government in check and was enacted in 1970.

The Rocky Flats plant was part of the United States' nuclear weapon production system with different components manufactured at various locations. The reason for this was to protect the program from being completely taken out by an enemy (i.e., Soviet) missile attack.

Some of the most critical component production plants were placed in the middle of the country, where a missile strike would be more difficult.

By the time the site was officially cleaned up in 2006, nearly 21 tons of weapons-grade plutonium, uranium, and americium were removed.

The process was painfully slow, fraught with inefficiencies and bureaucracy. One of the things I remember the most was having to go through the process of working with folks in charge of air quality, water quality, ecology, and a few other areas when someone wanted to dig a small hole in the buffer zone – a large zone established around the perimeter of the facility to prevent homes and businesses from being built too close to the facility. It was mostly open space and provided an excellent habitat for wildlife.

I mention this story because this is what it often feels like when you work for an enterprise company and want to try something new and untested.

This is why smaller, non-enterprise companies have a better chance of leading the way with recruitment marketing and employer branding.

They can be more nimble and test different ideas and concepts more easily. They also have to work harder on building awareness around their company and their roles. This can also lead to more testing and experimentation, which leads to new ideas, concepts, and, ultimately, a competitive advantage.

There are constraints involved with building a recruitment marketing and employer brand program within a smaller organization, including budget and people. But, constraints can be an unlikely benefit because it forces you to be more creative, which leads to breakthrough ideas.

With fewer people and resources, you'll need to lean on automation and other ways of driving efficiencies and scale with only a couple of people. You'll also be required to build cross-functional partnerships with your marketing team and leverage the talent and resources that already exist.

19

Conclusion

This Book is for Long-Term Focused Organizations

The ideas and recommendations in this book are *not* meant to become your sole strategy.

They're meant to be a guide and to spark ideas of your own.

I realize you have open roles you need to fill immediately, and you always will.

You'll need to continue executing your short-term tactics and strategies to attract and engage with people who are actively seeking another role.

You'll always need a combination of long-term and short-term strategies, just like any other marketing and sales teams.

However, what I've seen throughout my career in recruiting is a hole that is the long-term strategy.

I've been at companies who have tried, but they didn't have the right people in place to execute, and they weren't patient enough. They also didn't know what to measure and how to tell if what they were doing was working.

Many of these organizations were short-term focused at the top, which influenced how the rest of the organization operated.

My recommendations and ideas can be implemented in a publicly traded corporation or a hyper-growth focused startup, but it will be challenging. There's a reason many large companies outsource their digital marketing to agencies. It's expensive to build a team with all of the expertise needed.

Agencies have the expertise you need and can justify the cost by scaling their work across multiple clients.

What you'll find in this book will be best implemented within companies whose leaders value a long-term strategy. Whose leaders understand a solid business needs to look beyond the next quarter.

A sustainable, healthy, profitable business is one that will outlive everyone working there now. This kind of business is what our communities need now more than ever, and I hope this book will be part of the solution.

About the Author

Travis L. Scott is a strategic marketing consultant, coach, and writer, focusing on recruitment and talent acquisition. He started his career in recruiting at a boutique agency in Denver, CO, and eventually moved into a mix of contract and full-time corporate recruiting roles at Comcast, Cricket Wireless, Microsoft, and Booking.com.

In 2009, he began a digital marketing consulting side hustle, moving into this space full-time in 2014, eventually becoming the Director of Marketing in 2016 for one of his first clients, a B2B company in Denver, CO, where he remains as of the publishing of this book.

He has written for the employer brand sites of Microsoft and Dunkin' Brands and is a frequent contributor to the online media resource Recruiting Daily.

Travis lives in beautiful Spokane, WA with his wife, two sons, and two dogs.

You can connect with me on:
- http://travislscott.com
- https://twitter.com/509marketer
- https://linkedin.com/in/travisscott24

Printed in Great Britain
by Amazon